Greatly to Be PRAISED

Reflections for Thanksgiving & Advent

FROM THE BOOK OF PSALMS

Authors

Ali Shaw • Courtney Cohen • Jaime Hilton

Kat Lee • Kelli LaFram • Kelly Baker • Patti Brown

Hellomornings.org

TABLE OF CONTENTS

THE NEW Hellomornings BIBLE STUDY METHOD

We (The HelloMornings Team) are SO excited to share this new Bible study method with you!

The heart behind the method is "For Every Woman in Every Season." Whether you have 5 minutes or 50 minutes every morning, the HelloMornings study method can adapt to your schedule. We designed it so that a new believer won't feel overwhelmed and a seasoned Bible study student can dive deep into each passage.

We had three main goals in creating this method:

1. TO BUILD YOUR HABIT

Because building a daily God time habit is at the core of HelloMornings, we want to make sure you never feel overwhelmed with each day's study. If you only have 5 minutes, you can read the passage, write the verse and respond in a written prayer. If you have more time, you can dig deeper with one, two or all of the study "action steps." And if you want to go even deeper (or stretch the study out to a Saturday or Sunday) we are including group of study ideas in the front of the ebook so you'll always have a treasure trove of options to choose from.

2. TO BUILD YOUR GROUP

Our second goal was to create a method that encourages group interaction. Groups are integral to what we do here at HelloMornings. They are a way to build community, stay accountable to growth and learn from different perspectives.

But it's hard to find a group where everyone is at the same level of studying Scripture. That means with most Bible studies, some group members feel overwhelmed while others feel bored. Our goal is to bridge that gap and create content that not only fits any schedule, but also fits any level of study.

The beauty of this is that someone in your group who is brand new to the faith can daily dive into the same scriptures as a group leader who has been studying for decades. And the way we have formatted the content allows for each to learn and share in whatever way God is leading them so everyone can feel they have something to contribute, if they choose.

3. TO BUILD YOUR ROUTINE

In order to be the "hands and feet of Jesus," we need to:

1. Know Him—(God)
2. Understand His purpose for our lives—(Plan)
3. Follow His leading—(Move)

These are the core habits of HelloMornings.

God. Plan. Move.

Time with God is essential. And we believe that God has a purpose for each one of our lives. We also believe that He even has a purpose for each of our days. There are people He may want you to encourage today or ways He wants you to take action.

That is why we Plan. We want our daily planning to be done with His purposes in mind. Each daily worksheet has space for just a few of the most important tasks. Prayerfully planning is more powerful than any fancy productivity system because only God knows our heart, our purpose and our circumstances.

Finally, it's time to Move. This doesn't need to be a 3-mile run or a 25-minute workout. We simply want to be "fit for our calling"—i.e. have the energy to walk out the plan toward our purpose. If God has things He'd like us to do today, it's our responsibility to have the energy to do them. He does not give us more than we can handle.

For some, this might be simply drinking a morning glass of water. For others, it might be a short workout and for others it might be a healthy breakfast. The goal is just to do what we can to have the energy to respond to whatever God is calling us to each day. Kind of like an athlete makes sure to eat a good breakfast before a game so she has the energy to play well.

God. Plan. Move.

It doesn't need to take a long time. It could be as simple as a 5-minute routine of reading the daily passage, jotting down a few tasks and drinking a glass of water. Or it could be longer and more customized to your life.

Ultimately, we just want to start each day with the One who gave us all our days. And we want to plan our lives with the One who gives us our lives. And we want to Move wherever He may lead.

To a life well lived for the good of others and the glory of God,

The HelloMornings Team

SHARE THE STUDY

Will you consider helping us spread the word?

If you're in a HelloMornings group, invite all your group members to upgrade from the basic reading plan to this full study. It is well worth the price of a latte to study scripture deeply for 6 weeks and build a solid morning routine.

If you don't have a HelloMornings group, gather some friends together, send them to *HelloMornings.org/shop* to grab a copy of the study and spend the next 6 weeks journeying together! It's so much more fun and impactful when we learn and grow in community.

WAYS TO HELP OTHERS:

Use the hashtag *#HelloMornings* on Twitter or Instagram.

Share what you're learning on Facebook and link to *HelloMornings.org*

Tell your friends! Text, email or invite them to join you the next time you see them.

GET ALL THE RESOURCES:

We want to equip you to build a brilliant, God centered morning routine that leaves you feeling refueled and ready for action each day.

If you're not already on our email list, visit *HelloMornings.org* to download our free resources and receive our inspiring and idea-filled newsletter.

THE BIG BIBLE STUDY IDEA LIST

Each day of a HelloMornings study is filled with passages to read, a verse to write and plenty of action steps to take. But if you're ready to dive even deeper or you want to stretch our 5 day a week studies into 7 days, this list is the perfect way for you to add "tools" to your Bible study tool belt.

If you finish the study for the day and have more time, simply refer back to this "Big Bible Study Idea List" to select a few ways to dive even deeper into the passage you've been reading.

The best thing about this list is that it can be used on ANY section of scripture. So, if you want to do a study on 1 Corinthians 13 or look up all the verses on Faith, just use this list to build your own Bible study!

We want to equip you to study the Bible deeply regardless of whether you have a Bible study guide you're going through at the time or not. Try out each of these "tools" and add them to your Bible study "tool belt!"

READ AND WRITE

Ways to study scripture and dig deep into one passage.

READ

Simply read the passage. You can read it in your head, read out loud, read thoughtfully and slow, read in another translation.

WRITE

Honestly, this is my favorite way to start each morning. I *love* writing out scripture. There's something about the process of handwriting that both wakes me up and allows me to really marinate in the passage. It's also incredibly meaningful to have notebooks filled with handwritten scripture.

IDENTIFY KEY VERSES

In the passage you're reading, which verse holds the nugget of wisdom. Which verses explain the transformation of the main characters. Which verses speak most deeply to you in the season you're in right now?

HIGHLIGHT, UNDERLINE, BRACKET, CIRCLE, JOT

In this digital age, there is something therapeutic about words on a paper page and a pack of highlighters or colored pencils. I always loved looking at my grandmothers Bible filled with highlights, underlines, notes and circles.

Take time to circle commands, underline truths or highlight key verses in your favorite shade of pink. Bible study can be fun and colorful!

OBSERVE

Let your inner Nancy Drew loose. Uncover the 5 W's of the passage. Who, What, When, Where, Why and (don't forget) How. It's amazing how much we can learn from just naming the different elements of a passage or story.

ILLUSTRATE

In the margins of your Bible, or on a HelloMornings worksheet, get creative! Design word art focusing on a key point. Sketch the setting, characters or theme.

OUTLINE

Feeling more cerebral than creative? Outline the story or teaching. Highlight the main points and the sub-points to develop a greater understanding of where the author was coming from and what he was trying to communicate.

PERSONAL PARAPHRASE

Sometimes we learn best by teaching. Imagine you had to share the heart of the passage with a group of friends or a class of children, how would you paraphrase it? Or paraphrase it by incorporating your story into it and the things God has done in your life. You could even paraphrase it by simply incorporating your name in everywhere it has a generic pronoun.

QUESTIONS

Got questions? Just write them down. You can answer them later. Don't let your questions keep you from getting through the passage. Imagine you could interview the author, what would you ask?

RESPOND

A great way to dig deeper into scripture is to as a few simple questions. You can think about the answers as you read or you can write down your responses on the HelloMornings worksheet or in your own journal.

The Bible truly comes alive when we consider and pray about how God wants us to apply it to our own lives.

QUESTIONS TO CONSIDER:
- What does this say about God?
- What does this say about the church?
- What does this say about me?

- What truths are in this passage?
- Does this passage lead me to confess anything in prayer?
- What should I pray?
- What actions should I take?
- How can today be different because of this passage?
- What are some journaling questions?
- What is the lesson from this passage?
- Which key verse should I memorize this week?

RESEARCH

There is so much to be learned on every page of scripture. But sometimes we can take our study to a new level when we start flipping the pages and learning the "story behind the story."

Here are a few things you can research about the passage you are studying.

AUTHOR

Who wrote this passage? What do we know about him and how he fits into the story of the Bible? What were his circumstances? Why did he write it? Who was he writing to? Where was he when he wrote it? What had God done in his life to compel him to write this passage?

BACKGROUND

What was the background of the passage? What story or theme was introduced in previous verses or chapters of the book?

AUDIENCE

Who was the audience that the author was writing to? Why was it written to them? How do you think they responded to it? How would you have responded?

CONTEXT: CULTURAL, HISTORICAL, GRAMMATICAL

What was happening in history at the time the passage was written? What was the culture in which it was written like? How did the culture or the historical circumstances influence the author? Are there any grammatical rhythms or clues identifying or strengthening the authors meaning or ultimate intent?

CROSS REFERENCE

If you have a Bible with cross references (or using an online resource), look up all the verses associated with the passage. What can you learn from them and how do they influence the text?

COMMENTARIES

Read the commentary in your Bible, commentary books or at a trusted online source to gain even more insight into the passage.

TRANSLATIONS

Read the passage in multiple translations. How do they differ? How are they the same? What new truths can you glean from the variety of perspectives?

MAPS

Are there any maps in your Bible or online related to the passage you're studying? Follow the journey of the main characters. Look up modern day pictures of the locations. Research how long their journeys may have taken or any obstacles they may have encountered in their travels (culturally or geographically).

WORD STUDY (ORIGINAL LANGUAGE)

Brush up on your Greek and Hebrew and study the passage in the original language using an interlinear Bible.

READY TO DIVE IN?

Feel free to refer back to this list at any point, but now it's time to dive into the new HelloMornings study.

Here we go...

Cheering you on,

Kat Lee and the *HelloMornings.org* Team

Greatly to Be PRAISED

Reflections for Thanksgiving & Advent

FROM THE BOOK OF PSALMS

INTRODUCTION

IN THIS SEASON OF THANKSGIVING AND ADVENT, our hearts and minds are especially pointed toward God in gratitude, wonder, praise, and joy. Praise is due His name because of His steadfast love and great goodness! It is by His hand that we are led, cared for, protected, and saved. We have much to be thankful for. And it is only by Jesus' birth, death, and resurrection that we are offered eternal life. The world has great joy because our King has come!

Often at Thanksgiving, we look to the Book of Psalms to express our gratitude. The Book of Psalms is a lovely book of poetry that reflect many moods and offer us much teaching. These poems and songs, composed by a variety of writers long before Jesus' time, are an excellent way to join the original writers in praising God, praying prayers of gratitude, and discovering His help, guidance, and wisdom. We don't often look to the Psalms when celebrating Jesus' birth. But, because of the Messianic Psalms, these hymns are a wonderful way to rejoice in the advent of the Savior.

In this Bible study, we'll look intently into twenty-one psalms and use these ancient songs as a springboard to worship our God who is greatly to be praised. The first two parts of this study will focus on praise and thanksgiving and will walk us through the days leading to the Thanksgiving holiday. The third is a time of transition where we'll focus on God and His nature, as well as our need for a Savior. The final three parts of this study will walk us through a portion of Advent. In these parts, we'll focus on Messianic psalms that foretell the coming of Christ and give us information about His life and purpose. Two psalms are particularly rich and so we'll study them twice.

We'll spend time together in prayerful reflection and heartfelt gratitude. We'll focus on the miracle of Jesus' birth and His coming down from Heaven in the form of a precious child (both fully God and fully human) to save us from sin and reconcile us to a holy, righteous God. Together, we'll prepare our hearts to rejoice afresh!

Pray with me?

Oh, Lord, please open our hearts as we study these beautiful words of Scripture. Let us overflow in gratitude for who you are, all you've done for us, and all you've accomplished through the life of Christ our Savior. Without you, we have nothing, but with you, we have everything. You are our all in all. We ask that you use your Word to penetrate our hearts in new ways, take root, and grow much fruit for your Kingdom and for the glory of Jesus Christ. May we celebrate the birth of this small, sweet Savior and King of Kings in humble adoration and exalt your name forevermore. Thank you, God! You are *Greatly to be Praised!* Amen.

Ali

Note: This study would be beneficial any time of the year! But, if you'd like to do this study at Thanksgiving and Advent (like it was designed to be done) grab your calendar and look for Christmas day. Count back six weeks from Christmas and begin Part One of the study on Monday of that week. That way, when you get to Part Six, you'll be ending the study right at Christmastime. Blessings!

PART 1, DAY 1: PSALM 96

A LIGHT, COLD RAIN FELL ON US AS WE WAITED TO CROSS at the intersection of 100th St. and Central Park West in New York City. My daughter's eyes were sparkling with anticipation. Ever since she was four years old, she had been saying she wanted to live in New York City some day. Fifteen now, this was her first visit since she was an infant. We crossed the street. She set foot in Central Park and started twirling. Then the music poured out of her. She sang while she danced up and down paths and stairs and hills. The rain didn't matter. The people didn't matter. She was so overcome with joy there was no stopping her song.

Have you experienced joy like that? Been so overwhelmed by the goodness of God that you couldn't help sing His praises? The title of our study comes from verse 4 of Psalm 96—*"for great is the Lord, and **greatly to be praised.**"* Psalm 96 is like a giant celebration. You can almost see the world rejoicing…tree limbs raised to the heavens, little bird mouths open in riotous harmony, the steady rhythm of ocean waves laying the beat for creation's praise song to the Lord.

When you experience something wonderful, don't you just want to tell someone? The greatness of God not only leads His people to rejoice but also to tell others. David Dockery writes of Psalm 96, *"The Lord God of Israel rules over all the earth, and all its peoples must bow to Him. This is the great missionary song of the Bible."* Declare, ascribe, say. These active verbs remind us that we are to be active in our faith, not only with our hands and feet, but with our mouths. Our praise song is meant to be heard!

God is to be honored and praised because He is the Lord who made the heavens, in splendor and majesty, in strength and beauty. He is the one who comes to judge the earth in righteousness. What a tender mystery it is that today we know that this great and glorious Lord has indeed come… come as a tiny babe who would fill our hearts to overflowing with hope and thankfulness.

Today just praise Him. When you struggle, praise Him. When you are happy, praise Him. When you don't know what to do next, praise Him. Make today be an exercise in praise and see what He does in your heart. For He is great, and greatly to be praised!

— KEY VERSE —

Sing to the Lord, bless his name; tell of his salvation from day to day. (Psalm 96:2)

Hellomornings

God. Plan. Move.

GOD TIME

READ : Psalm 96
WRITE : Psalm 96:2

. . . .

. . . .

. . . .

REFLECT :
- List all the commands in Psalm 96.
- Read 1 Chronicles 16:7-36 and note similarities with Psalm 96.
- According to this psalm, **why** is God to be praised?
- Do you find it easy or challenging to *"declare his glory"* (v. 3)? How can you grow in this area?
- Spend time just praising God. No requests, no confessions, just praise. If you are struggling with praise, play "Revelation Song" by Kari Jobe (you can find it on YouTube).

RESPOND :

. . . .

. . . .

. . . .

. . . .

. . . .

PLAN TIME

THINGS TO DO (3-5 MAX) :

KEY EVENTS TODAY :

MOVE TIME

MORNING WATER ☐

B : _____
L : _____
D : _____

SNACK :

SIMPLE WORKOUT ☐

PART 1, DAY 2: PSALM 121

I WAS NINETEEN YEARS OLD, standing in front of the Métro ticket vending machine at the Charles de Gaulle Airport in Paris, when a young man approached, offering help in accented English. I had just arrived, having flown alone from the US, and had a day to kill until my train to Florence, Italy left that night. We chatted for a few minutes, then he offered a different solution to my travel challenges: *"I can drive you to the city. My car is right outside."* I have no idea what I was thinking, but I said, *"Okay!"* and hopped into a total stranger's car in a foreign city. I spent the entire day with him. We drove all over the city, visited famous Parisian spots, ate several meals together. The mind can go to dark places thinking of what might have happened. But *"the Lord is my keeper."* He *"neither slumbers nor sleeps."* He kept my *"going out"* and my *"coming in"* that day. He kept me *"from...evil,"* as Psalm 121 says. The young man dropped me off and waved goodbye in the evening, and I never saw him again.

It is just so easy to trust ourselves and our systems isn't it? We make plans, we set up safeguards. We think we can manage it all. But challenges and even dangers surround us, some of our own choosing (like my risky Parisian adventure) and many we don't see coming. The sun beats down on us whether we want it to or not. But the Lord is our shade from the scorching heat of life. The cool shade of His protection refreshes.

Psalm 121 is the second of fifteen psalms labeled *Song of Ascents.* The generally accepted view of the psalms that were labeled thus is that they were hymns sung during pilgrimages to Jerusalem. Imagine how comforting this psalm would have been to those singing it on a long hot journey up to the holy city!

"The very mountains to which they travel symbolize that surrounding care for those who journey where God sends. We go our own way at our own risk." –R.E.O. White

Your heavenly Father watches over you day and night, guarding your soul. Does this mean bad things will never happen? Of course not, because sin is in the world. God's protection at times does extend to physical protection here on earth, as it did for a good-judgment-challenged nineteen year old girl in Paris. But we can always trust God to guard our **souls** for eternity, or as the psalm says, *"from this time forth and forevermore."* Rejoice with thanksgiving for God's eternal protection today!

—  —

My help comes from the Lord, who made heaven and earth. (Psalm 121:2)

Hellomornings

God. Plan. Move.

READ : Psalm 121
WRITE : Psalm 121:2

· ·

· ·

· ·

REFLECT :
- According to this psalm, what are the ways God helps you?
- Read Psalm 46:1, Isaiah 41:10, Hebrews 4:16 and add to your list of ways God helps.
- Underline each instance of the word "keep." What does it mean that the Lord keeps you?
- The Lord who protects also refreshes. In what ways has God refreshed you and been "your shade on your right hand" (v. 5)?
- Journal about a time you experienced God's help and protection.

RESPOND :

· ·

· ·

· ·

· ·

· ·

PLAN TIME

THINGS TO DO (3-5 MAX) :

KEY EVENTS TODAY :

MOVE TIME

MORNING WATER ☐

B : _____

L : _____

D : _____

SNACK :

SIMPLE WORKOUT ☐

PART 1, DAY 3: PSALM 130

"DID IT COME?" She didn't have to say a word—my daughter's anxious eyes asked the question as I checked my email for the cast list. She and her younger brother perform with a musical theater group in our city and had been waiting for weeks to find out what their newest roles would be. She knew the cast list would come, *"It has to!"* But when, and what it might tell her, she knew not.

Have you waited like that? Knowing something you desperately wanted would come, but not when? Thousands of years ago, the night watchmen of Jerusalem stood on the thick wall to watch over their city, eyes on the horizon, knowing that the coming of the sun would mean the end of their shift. They never questioned that the sun would rise, just as we don't. The repetition in verse 6 underscores and emphasizes the truth that our soul's confidence can be even greater in the Lord's coming than in the rising of the sun!

Like yesterday's psalm, Psalm 130 is a Song of Ascent, possibly sung on the pilgrimage journey up to Jerusalem. I picture the people with their eyes on the horizon like the watchmen, walking toward the holy city, confident in the hope His word gives—hope for forgiveness, for redemption. A crowd of people of all shapes and sizes, His temple their destination, secure in His steadfast love, on a journey toward renewal through offering sacrifice at the altar.

You and I are on a journey too, aren't we? We are journeying as aliens and strangers through this earthly life, our destination-His arms in eternity. Sometimes the journey feels like standing still. When life overwhelms, it can seem like the pain is insurmountable. Our sins pile up like a mountain in whose depths we are buried. Paralyzed, we can do nothing but cry out and wait. Friend, your hope is never misplaced when your hope is in the Lord. The promised Messiah was the most precious gift, the ultimate and final sacrifice, born out of His steadfast love for His people. Through Jesus, the incomprehensible freedom and joy of forgiveness breaks you free from the depths of the graveyard of your sins.

And what of my young waiting actress? The cast list came, at last. As did the screams and tears of joy when she learned that she was cast in the lead role she had hoped for. The rejoicing that a teenage girl so easily enters into is a mere shadow of the heavenly exultation that our hearts and souls were made for! We wait for Him with the hope and confidence that only our faithful and loving Lord deserves.

—  KEY VERSE —

I wait for the Lord, my soul waits, and in his word I hope. (Psalm 130:5)

Hellomornings

God. Plan. Move.

GOD TIME

READ : Psalm 130
WRITE : Psalm 130:5

. . . .

. . . .

. . . .

REFLECT :
- What promises can you find in today's passage?
- Why hope in God's Word? See Psalm 119:105, 2 Timothy 3:16-17, Hebrews 4:12.
- Research the role of the watchmen in ancient Israel.
- Read Psalm 25:3, Psalm 33:20, Proverbs 20:22, Isaiah 25:9. Why can you confidently wait?
- Do you need to ask the Lord for forgiveness in an area? Spend time today in prayerful discussion about this part of your life with your heavenly Father.

RESPOND :

. . . .

. . . .

. . . .

. . . .

. . . .

PLAN TIME

THINGS TO DO (3-5 MAX) :

KEY EVENTS TODAY :

MOVE TIME

MORNING WATER ☐

B : _____

L : _____

D : _____

SNACK :

SIMPLE WORKOUT ☐

THE BACK DOOR SLAMMED OPEN. *"Mama! Hurry! A chicken is stuck in the barbed wire!"* I threw my feet into my farm boots and raced down the backstairs, following my son. *"There!"* he pointed as we ran to the bird hanging upside down from a fence. The hen had somehow gotten her foot entangled in the fence wire, then flipped over in her struggle. Other chickens surrounded her, pecking at her head and neck. We shooed them away and got to work cutting the bloodied hen out of the wire that entrapped her. We whispered gently and stroked her to calm her as we twisted and pulled and cut as carefully as we could. At last she was free—in rough shape, but liberated and still alive.

I have felt like a chicken hanging upside down, trapped in a barbed wire fence, and getting her eyes pecked at. I'll bet you have as well. Sometimes life is just hard and painful. Sometimes in our efforts to free ourselves from the troubles we are stuck in, we make things worse. And sometimes the people we think of as friends hurt us. The author of today's passage surely felt that way too. *"The snares of death encompassed me; the pangs of Sheol laid hold on me; I suffered distress and anguish."* (Psalm 116:3)

Much like the hen who squawked for help, we cry out to the One who can deliver us from our distress, as the psalmist does in verse 4: *"O Lord, I pray, deliver my soul!"* My son might not have heard that little bird's cry, but you can count on the truth that God always hears you. *"Call to me and I will answer you, and will tell you great and hidden things that you have not known."* (Jeremiah 33:3) Rest your mind on this for a moment: The creator of the Universe, all-powerful, all-knowing, the great I AM… He is the One who hears and answers you. My heart cries out in thanksgiving for His mercy! *"what is man that you are mindful of him, and the son of man that you care for him?"* (Psalm 8:4)

We nursed our little hen back to health. She spent time safely away from the other chickens until she healed. From then on, she was deeply attached to us, running to us when we went outside, perfectly happy to be picked up and carried around. She knew that the hands that had delivered and healed her were trustworthy. How much more so are the hands of our Lord, who has delivered us and healed us for eternity! Today, settle your heart to rest in those loving hands, thankful for His mercy and tender care.

—  KEY VERSE —

I love the Lord, because he has heard my voice and my pleas for mercy. (Psalm 116:1)

Hellomornings

God. Plan. Move.

READ : Psalm 116:1-9
WRITE : Psalm 116:1

....

....

....

REFLECT :
- Reread Psalm 116:1-9. Why does the psalmist love the Lord?
- Make a list of the things this passage tells you about God's nature.
- What happens when you call on the Lord according to this psalm? Add thoughts from Psalm 50:15, Psalm 86:5, Romans 10:13.
- Write out Psalm 116:7 and Matthew 11:28. Meditate on the rest God offers.
- What has the Lord delivered you from?

RESPOND :

....

....

....

....

....

PLAN TIME

THINGS TO DO (3-5 MAX) :

KEY EVENTS TODAY :

MOVE TIME

MORNING WATER ☐

B : _____

L : _____

D : _____

SNACK :

SIMPLE WORKOUT ☐

PART 1, DAY 5: PSALM 116:10-19

I LAY ON THE COUCH PERFECTLY STILL. I felt like I was evaporating, slowly disappearing. My baby had died. The painful days played in my mind… no heartbeat, hemorrhaging, emergency surgery… now that I was home and recovering, the grief and physical trauma immobilized me. *"Rejoice always, pray without ceasing, give thanks in all circumstances; for this is the will of God in Christ Jesus for you."* (1 Thessalonians 5:16-18) It was impossible. I was sure I would never rejoice or give thanks again. My heart was too broken.

Yesterday we studied the first half of Psalm 116, where the psalmist extolled God's goodness for delivering him from death. His response to God's mercy is the subject of today's passage. In Psalm 116:17 he says he *will offer to you the sacrifice of thanksgiving and call on the name of the Lord."* In ancient Israel, the thank offering (a type of peace offering) was different from the guilt offering. It was given not out of obligation, but out of an abundance of love and gratitude. William Smith wrote, *"The general principle of the peace offering seems to have been that it should be entirely spontaneous, offered as occasion should arise, from the feeling of the sacrificer himself."* To offer it, one had to have already offered the guilt offering, and be in right standing with God. Those who believe in Jesus Christ have been made in right standing with God already through the blood of Jesus' sacrifice on the cross—we are free to give a sacrifice of thanksgiving at any time.

A sacrifice is not a sacrifice without a cost, is it? As Christians, we are not required to bear the financial cost of sacrificing at the temple. Jesus' sacrifice did away with that need. For you and me, the sacrifice of thanksgiving will often come out of the pain in our lives. When the circumstances of life are pleasant, it is easy to give thanks. But when we suffer, thankfulness is harder to come by. Your sacrifice of thanksgiving is not dependent on your circumstances but on your understanding of the goodness of God. It is not based on what is happening but on Who He is.

God is patient. It took months for me to be able to see through my grief-stricken spiritual fog. Even now, seventeen years later, I remember how difficult it was to finally pray that prayer of thanksgiving after losing our baby. It genuinely felt like a sacrifice but one I undertook out of love for Him and obedience to His will. Because of His tender love, I experienced a deep sense of freedom and healing after praying. Today, ask God to help you be thankful in the painful circumstances of your life. *"The one who offers thanksgiving as his sacrifice glorifies me; to one who orders his way rightly I will show the salvation of God!"* (Psalm 50:23)

— KEY VERSE —

I will offer to you the sacrifice of thanksgiving and call on the name of the Lord. (Psalm 116:17)

Hellomornings

God. Plan. Move.

READ : Psalm 116:10-19
WRITE : Psalm 116:17

. . . .

. . . .

. . . .

REFLECT :
- Paraphrase today's passage in your own words.
- Verse 12 asks how to respond to God's blessing. What is the answer according to this psalm?
- Research the purpose of the thank offering and its significance. Leviticus 7:11-17 is a good place to start.
- How does Hebrews 13:15 complement Psalm 116:17?
- Write 1 Thessalonians 5:16-18. In what areas are you struggling to give thanks?

RESPOND :

. . . .

. . . .

. . . .

. . . .

. . . .

PLAN TIME

THINGS TO DO (3-5 MAX) :

KEY EVENTS TODAY :

MOVE TIME

MORNING WATER ☐

B : _____

L : _____

D : _____

SNACK :

SIMPLE WORKOUT ☐

PART 2, DAY 1: PSALM 66:1-9

HAVE YOU EVER FELT AN OVERWHELMING JOY THAT LEADS YOU TO SHOUT?

When my husband and I began dating, we spent football season glued to the TV. Before Steve came into my life, I couldn't have cared less about professional sports. But, in my longing to be near him, I gradually developed an interest. This interest took on a voice when I began shouting at the players through my TV screen. I was an important part of the game, there in my living room. And yet, the few times I've watched games live in a stadium, I've pondered the smallness of me. In the midst of such a grand crowd, with far more flamboyant fans, what difference does my shout make? In the face of such insignificant smallness, why bother vocalizing my excitement? Then again, if every person in the crowd focused solely on their own insignificance, there would be no cheering crowd, no noise to unsettle or confuse the enemy, no 12th man to support the team.

In our passage today, there's an incredible emphasis on praise—loud, unashamed, vocalized praise. Here, the psalmist recalls the Exodus miracle when more than a million Hebrew slaves walked through the Red Sea on dry land. Throughout Scripture, the Lord calls His people to praise from a place of remembrance. There is power in remembering what God has done. Our faith builds as we see what God has done in the past and believe in what He can and will do in our future.

Psalm 66 is a testimony of praise—recalling those miracles God had performed more than 400 years earlier. This ongoing testimony and ongoing praise fuels the faith of God's people. More than that, we see in this passage that not only do the people of God praise Him, but all of creation does as well. Even His enemies "come cringing" to Him because of His immense power. God's works are so incredible that they cannot be ignored.

During this Thanksgiving week, let this be a time to remember how the Lord has delivered us from impossible circumstances and how He has shown up faithfully. Let this looking back, this remembrance, be a catalyst pushing us forward to rejoice in the promises we have yet to see fulfilled.

— **KEY VERSE** —

Come and see what God has done; he is awesome in his deeds toward the children of man. (Psalm 66:5)

Hellomornings

God. Plan. Move.

GOD TIME

READ : Psalm 66:1-9
WRITE : Psalm 66:5

. . . .

. . . .

. . . .

REFLECT :
- Highlight or underline the praise action words (ex: shout, sing, worship, etc.).
- Read Exodus 14:21 through 15:21 and compare it to today's passage.
- Write down at least three ways God has provided for you and praise Him as you remember.
- Consider the various ways of praising shown in this passage. Ask God about ways He would love to see you worship Him, perhaps even a way that isn't normal or easy for you.
- Memorize today's key verse.

RESPOND :

. . . .

. . . .

. . . .

. . . .

. . . .

PLAN TIME

THINGS TO DO (3-5 MAX) :

KEY EVENTS TODAY :

MOVE TIME

MORNING WATER ☐

B : _____
L : _____
D : _____

SNACK :

SIMPLE WORKOUT ☐

PART 2, DAY 2: PSALM 66:10-20

WHEN I WAS ELEVEN, MY FAMILY FACED FORECLOSURE and had to vacate our home in less than 24 hours. Everything swiftly went into storage where it sat for the year we lived with two sets of grandparents. Our time without a home of our own required us to move from Houston to Fort Worth, from one set of grandparents to another until my parents found their feet to stand on again. With little to call mine, Christmas came in March when we finally found a rental home and were reunited with our stored possessions. I hadn't understood the difference between want and need until that year of lack. I didn't consider the abundance I had until I experienced lack. And for those lessons, I thank God to this day.

Verses 10 through 12 describe difficult and challenging circumstances that God allowed. *"You have tried us as silver is tried."* (v. 10) How is silver tried? Through fire that causes impurities to rise to the top. Despite affliction and pain, we still have reason to give thanks through testing and trials. God allows many of these for our ultimate abundance, an abundance that is wholly dependent on Him. While in the first half of Psalm 66, praise stems from a place of joyful remembrance, the second half reveals praise that emerges purified, having remembered the hard times God brought the psalmist through.

The heart of this psalm also recognizes that we have things to give and things to give up. We can give offerings of worship—all the more precious when they are sacrifices of praise—and we can bring our best to the Lord. We can keep our words of promise and intention to Him and vocalize not only our praises and blessings, but also our cries, and He will hear and respond. Yet beyond the giving, we must also give up. We must release our iniquities, refusing to cherish those bents towards sin in our hearts.

When our expectations and comforts get interrupted, we can trust that God had a better plan all along. Though it can be frustrating in the moment to see those expectations falter and fail, we can learn to believe that God is bringing us out to a place of abundance. He is always greater than our circumstances.

— KEY VERSE —

Come and hear, all you who fear God, and I will tell what he has done for my soul. (Psalm 66:16)

Hellomornings

God. Plan. Move.

READ : Psalm 66:10-20
WRITE : Psalm 66:16

. . . .

. . . .

REFLECT :
- Write down three ways the Lord has delivered you through adversity into abundance.
- Spend a few moments in worship, thanking Him for the adversity as well as the abundance.
- Meditate on Psalm 66:16. What story can you tell about what God has done for your soul?
- Ask God for one person you can share your story with about how God moved in those situations.
- Ask God to reveal His abundance to you in the midst of any adversity you currently face.

RESPOND :

. . . .

. . . .

. . . .

. . . .

PLAN TIME

THINGS TO DO (3-5 MAX) :

KEY EVENTS TODAY :

MOVE TIME

MORNING WATER ☐

B : _____

L : _____

D : _____

SNACK :

SIMPLE WORKOUT ☐

PART 2, DAY 3: PSALM 145:1-13

THE DAY LEADING UP TO THANKSGIVING IS OFTEN A HURRIED ONE. People hurry to the store for the last critical ingredient they forgot earlier that week. Cooks hurry through baking and prepping, hosts hurry through cleaning and decorating, travelers hurry to visit family at overnight destinations. Food and décor take the focus. The event takes precedence.

During the several times I've hosted Thanksgiving, I've gotten swept up in the rush. I've sought perfection in the presentation rather than seeking to present my guests with true perfection—the Giver worthy of our thanks.

Today's psalm draws us back to the presence of perfection. In thirteen verses, we see three elements of focus: God's name (*who* He is), God's works (*what* He does), and God's kingdom (*where* He dwells). This psalm of praise beckons us back to dwell on His beauty, His power, and His presence. Our dwelling on Him requires a stillness within our souls. And that stillness opens the way for the Lord to transform our bent towards hurry into peace amidst the storm.

Driving to my women's Bible study one day, I spent my few moments alone in worship: praising God out loud, singing to Him of His goodness, submitting my heart and my day to Him. My heart overflowed with His peace and presence as I parked and walked inside to meet with friends. One lovely lady commented on my face that day, how it glowed, how she could see the manifestation of peace in my countenance.

Don't we often describe a pregnant woman's face as "glowing"? Although I wasn't physically pregnant then, my soul was pregnant with life, eager to share, eager to birth the beauty God placed in me that morning. This psalm is pregnant with that same life, filled with an eagerness to display the glory of God by pointing to His name, works, and kingdom.

When we take time to bask in the presence of God, others take notice. Beauty and peace overtake our countenance, despite the circumstances of the day. This Thanksgiving, along with you, I plan on presenting the beauty of the perfect One more than a perfect presentation on my table. Let's take time to dwell with Him, to gaze on His beauty, to place the focus rightly back on the Giver worthy of all our thanks.

—  KEY VERSE —

Great is the Lord, and greatly to be praised, and his greatness is unsearchable. (Psalm 145:3)

Hellomornings

God. Plan. Move.

READ : Psalm 145:1-13
WRITE : Psalm 145:3

. . . .

. . . .

. . . .

REFLECT :
- In one color, highlight every word describing God's personhood and *name* in today's passage.
- In a second color, highlight every word describing God's *works*.
- In a third color, highlight every word describing God's *kingdom*.
- Write down aspects of God, His works, and His kingdom for which you are thankful.
- Ask the Lord if there is anything on your to-do list today that you can release.

RESPOND :

. . . .

. . . .

. . . .

. . . .

. . . .

PLAN TIME

THINGS TO DO (3-5 MAX) :

KEY EVENTS TODAY :

MOVE TIME

MORNING WATER ☐

B : _____

L : _____

D : _____

SNACK :

SIMPLE WORKOUT ☐

PART 2, DAY 4: PSALM 145:14-21

MY TYPICAL THANKSGIVING DAY EXPECTATIONS: having freshly baked muffins and coffee while we watch the parade with the kids, a slow cooking process to enjoy with family and friends filling the kitchen to help, taking turns to share thanks while lingering over the meal, football to watch and enjoy, and leftovers to nibble on throughout the day while we simply relax.

What usually ends up happening: too much time and effort spent making a magical breakfast wears me out before the real cooking begins, the parade bores me ten minutes in, my husband roasts the turkey and I cook everything else while the kids play, we forget to go around the table because we're focused on preparing our children's plates, and I end up grateful for leftovers because I'm tired of cooking for the next week.

Is the *idea* of something ever better than the *experience* for you? Disappointment can sneak up on us when we have unmet expectations. But the Lord lays out clearly in His Word what we can expect of Him. And, even more, He shows how we can come to Him with expectancy. His ways often turn out differently than we may anticipate, but He never fails.

Today's passage reveals four ways God relates to us in His goodness and each way points to how close He is. In Him, we experience His salvation, His provision, His nearness, and His protection. What God does flows from who He is. He is righteous and kind. He is the God who sees—sees our needs and weaknesses and desires. He is a good Father who enjoys the presence of His children.

So, what can we do in response to His goodness? We give thanks. We open our mouths to speak praises, to bless Him. How can we possibly bless God, the One who blesses us? If you have children, have they ever told you how much they love you? Or how they love having you as a mommy? How does that make you feel? Blessed, right? We have the opportunity to bless our perfect Father by speaking our love, by giving thanks for who He is and how He moves in our lives.

Today, let's set down our expectations of a perfect holiday and enter with hearts of expectancy, enjoying all the blessings He gives.

—  KEY VERSE —

The Lord is near to all who call on him, to all who call on him in truth. (Psalm 145:18)

Hellomornings

God. Plan. Move.

READ : Psalm 145:14-21
WRITE : Psalm 145:18

. . . .

. . . .

. . . .

REFLECT :
- Consider God's salvation, provision, nearness, and protection, and write down ways you have experienced these during the past week, month, or year.
- Memorize today's key verse.
- Begin a gratitude journal (or add to an existing one) where you can record daily blessings.
- Ask God to make you aware that He is near to you today.
- Listen to the song "Be Near" by Shane and Shane.

RESPOND :

. . . .

. . . .

. . . .

. . . .

. . . .

PLAN TIME

THINGS TO DO (3-5 MAX) :

KEY EVENTS TODAY :

MOVE TIME

MORNING WATER ☐

B : _____

L : _____

D : _____

SNACK :

SIMPLE WORKOUT ☐

PART 2, DAY 5: PSALM 100

DO YOU REMEMBER WHEN BLACK FRIDAY ACTUALLY BEGAN ON FRIDAY MORNING rather than on Thursday afternoon? When the entirety of Thanksgiving Day held a sacred aspect—set apart for family and feasting and football? Leaving homes in the black, predawn hours, determined shoppers geared up to gain an advantage over their Christmas shopping lists. They trudged through traffic, stood in nearly eternal lines, and eventually attained their goal. Today, it can be tempting to begin Black Friday on Thursday out of fear that we'll miss out on something we've had our eyes on.

Sometimes, the lure of temporal gain tempts us to shortchange what has far more eternal value. And, what could possibly have more value than God and people?

Today's passage is all about praise. But right in the center of this short psalm we find the key to the center of our praise: *"Know that the Lord, he is God! It is he who made us, and we are his; we are his people...."* (v. 3) While praise is beautiful when it comes from grateful hearts which acknowledge all that God has done in our lives, praise becomes truly *powerful* when it centers upon this: knowing who God is, who we are, and whose we are.

Who is God? He is the pinnacle. He is truly the Beginning and the End. And this one and only God created people. We can never grasp who we are as creatures until we know who our Creator is. Genesis 1:27 says, *"So God created man in his own image, in the image of God he created him; male and female he created them."* As image-bearers of God, we have the privilege and responsibility to bear His image throughout the world, in our own circles of influence. God is *God*. God, the Creator, created *us*. And, He calls us His own—His *people*.

When we live knowing who God is, who we are, and whose we are, we are able to praise powerfully. As He guides us, we gain eyes to see more of who He is and how He moves. We can recognize His goodness, His steadfast love, and His faithfulness. This way of seeing helps us see what is sacred, what is worthy of praise.

— KEY VERSE —

Know that the Lord, he is God! It is he who made us, and we are his; we are his people, and the sheep of his pasture. (Psalm 100:3)

Hellomornings

God. Plan. Move.

READ : Psalm 100
WRITE : Psalm 100:3

. . . .

. . . .

. . . .

REFLECT :
- Memorize today's key verse.
- Write down as many words as you can think of to describe who God is.
- Ask God, "What do you want to show me today about who You are and who I am?" Listen for His response.
- Read Psalm 100. How do worship, gratitude, and joy relate to each other?
- Ask God, "How can I follow You today?" Write down what you sense He is saying.

RESPOND :

. . . .

. . . .

. . . .

. . . .

. . . .

PLAN TIME

THINGS TO DO (3-5 MAX) :

MOVE TIME

MORNING WATER ☐

B : _____

L : _____

D : _____

KEY EVENTS TODAY :

SNACK :

SIMPLE WORKOUT ☐

PART 3, DAY 1: PSALM 24

THE ESV GIVES PSALM 24 THE TITLE "THE KING OF GLORY." The NKJV titles it "The King of Glory and His Kingdom." Who is the *King of Glory*? In these 10 verses we see that the King of Glory is our Creator (vv. 1-2), that He is holy (vv. 3-6), and that He is a Divine Warrior (vv. 7-10).

It's easy to skim over the first two verses of this chapter. As Christians, we've heard many times that God created the whole universe. This isn't anything new to us, but it shouldn't be any less amazing. In the beginning, God simply spoke, and the things He wanted to exist came into existence. God's words alone bring creation into being which showcases His glory.

Not only is He a glorious creator, He is glorious in His holiness, meaning He is absolutely perfect in every way. So perfect, in fact, that only those with clean hands and pure hearts can come into His presence. People who not only do right, but do right for the right reason, are able to ascend to where He is. On our own, we cannot come to Him. We do not act right all the time, and when we do, our motives are not always pure. Only One is perfect in action and motives—Jesus. And it is through our faith in Him that we, too, are seen by God as having clean hands and a pure heart.

He is glorious Creator, He is glorious in holiness, and He is glorious in might. He is Lord of Hosts, and has all of creation at His command. He is the Divine Warrior who has blessed, vindicated, and made righteous those who seek His face—those who desire Him above all else.

He is the King of glory, whose majesty and splendor are displayed in His love for us. Yes, He created the universe. Yes, He is perfect in all His ways. Yes, He is all powerful and mighty. Yet He wants us. And it is through His glorious grace that we begin to search for Him, find Him and enjoy His glory. He is greatly to be praised!

Lord in Heaven, King of glory, all of earth belongs to you. You are perfect in all your ways. You are powerful and mighty. You are worthy of all our worship and adoration. You alone deserve to be loved, yet you love us. You are the God of our salvation. You are greatly to be praised. Amen.

— KEY VERSE —

He will receive blessing from the Lord and righteousness from the God of his salvation. Such is the generation of those who seek him, who seek the face of the God of Jacob. Selah. (Psalm 24:5-6)

Hellomornings

God. Plan. Move.

READ : Psalm 24
WRITE : Psalm 24:5-6

....

....

....

REFLECT :
- Read the history of creation in Genesis 1:1-2:7.
- Read 1 Samuel 2:2, 1 Peter 1:15-16, and 1 John 1:7. What do these verses tell us about the holiness of God?
- God is our Divine Warrior. Does this title remind you of any Old Testament stories?
- Write a prayer glorifying God as Creator, for His holiness, and for being your personal Warrior.
- Do you have questions about this psalm? Share them with your HM group or a trusted friend.

RESPOND :

....

....

....

....

PLAN TIME

THINGS TO DO (3-5 MAX) :

KEY EVENTS TODAY :

MOVE TIME

MORNING WATER ☐

B : _____

L : _____

D : _____

SNACK :

SIMPLE WORKOUT ☐

PART 3, DAY 2: PSALM 63

NOT TOO LONG AGO I FOUND MYSELF IN A WILDERNESS PLACE. I wouldn't have described it as wilderness, more like just plain chaos. I was working, raising children, taking care of the home, and supporting my husband as he finished grad school. It was busy and what I thought I needed—what I longed for—was the opportunity to quit my job and stay home. That would relieve some of the chaos and feeling of being overwhelmed; I just knew it. So I begged and prayed and finally my prayer was answered.

My husband graduated and took a job that supported our family. I was able to stay home. I could take a breath. The weight would be lifted off my shoulders… or so I thought.

David writes Psalm 63 in the wilderness of Judah while running from those who sought his life—either Saul (1 Samuel 24) or his son, Absalom (2 Samuel 15:13-30), we're not sure which. I'm sure there were times when David just wanted to quit running. I'm sure there were moments when he thought, "If I could just settle down at home and live a peaceful life I would be happy—I could take a breath." But this Psalm reveals that if those moments existed, they didn't last. David knew what his soul really craved.

Just like David, our souls eagerly desire our faithful Almighty God. We need Him more than water, food, escape from our enemies, or the opportunity to stay home with our children. God's lovingkindness is better than any kind of life we can imagine, which is why David earnestly sought God early in the morning.

It didn't take long after I became a stay-at-home-mom that I began to understand that my circumstances are not what brings joy. It is only fellowship with my Savior that can bring calm delight to my weary soul. It is through the earnest, diligent, and sometimes painstaking search and praise of my God that my soul finds the cool drink of water and the tasty morsel that it longs for.

Lord, you alone are what my soul needs. I thirst and hunger for you. Fellowship with you, my Creator and Savior, is what brings me joy no matter the circumstances. Thank you for teaching this to me and drawing me near to you. Please stir in me an even greater desire to seek you each morning. Amen.

— KEY VERSE —

O God, you are my God; earnestly I seek you; my soul thirsts for you; my flesh faints for you, as in a dry and weary land where there is no water. (Psalm 63:1)

Hellomornings

God. Plan. Move.

READ : Psalm 63
WRITE : Psalm 63:1

. . . .

. . . .

. . . .

REFLECT :
- Pray Psalm 63 aloud to your Savior.
- Do a word study for *seek*. How does this help you better understand the psalm?
- Recite the Hello Mornings theme verse, Psalm 143:8, several times.
- List three (or more) reasons the psalmist gives for seeking the Lord early in the morning.
- Do you have questions about this psalm? Share them with your HM group or a trusted friend.

RESPOND :

. . . .

. . . .

. . . .

. . . .

. . . .

PLAN TIME

THINGS TO DO (3-5 MAX) :

KEY EVENTS TODAY :

MOVE TIME

MORNING WATER ☐

B : _____
L : _____
D : _____

SNACK :

SIMPLE WORKOUT ☐

PART 3, DAY 3: PSALM 130

"IF YOU, LORD, SHOULD MARK INIQUITIES, O LORD, WHO COULD STAND?" (v. 3) Not many. Actually, not any. Certainly, not me! However, for the longest time, I tried to stand on my own two feet and prove my worth to my Maker. Like so many Christians, I wrongly believed that I was expected to keep all the "rules" of Christian living and *earn* a ticket into heaven.

The psalmist knew otherwise. He knew that he needed mercy, so he cried out for it. He knew he needed forgiveness, so relied on it. He knew he needed a Messiah—the promised deliverer, Savior, and Redeemer, so he waited for Him.

When these verses were written, Jesus hadn't yet been born as a helpless infant and placed in a manger. The story of Jesus' humble, servant life on earth hadn't yet unfolded. The Redemption story had not reached its climax. But the psalmist confidently hoped for salvation just the same.

His hope wasn't wishful thinking. It wasn't some "cross your fingers and hope for the best" hope. No, the psalmist's hope was rooted in Yahweh, the one true God. The psalmist confidently placed His trust in his Master and waited for Him to come through. God had promised salvation from sin and the psalmist believed Him at His word.

When I finally realized that there was nothing I could do to earn God's love and forgiveness, I was broken and healed all at the same time. My pride was shattered, but my soul was redeemed. No, none can stand before God unless we have an Advocate standing with us—an Advocate who says, "I lived a perfect life for her. I took the punishment for her flawed and sinful living. I love her. She is mine. She is forgiven."

Do you know what is the most amazing thing? God sent this Advocate. It was all planned out from before the beginning. The psalmist knew Jesus was coming. We know He came. Now, like the psalmist, we can live in the hope of salvation, rejoice in His mercy, and tell others of His abundant redemption.

O Lord, if you should mark iniquities who could stand? Only those standing with Jesus. Thank you for your mercy, your forgiveness, and your Son our Redeemer. You are greatly to be praised! Amen.

—  KEY VERSE —

I wait for the Lord, my soul waits, and in his word I hope. (Psalm 130:5)

Hellomornings

God. Plan. Move.

GOD TIME

READ : Psalm 130
WRITE : Psalm 130:5

. . . .

. . . .

REFLECT :
 – Read Genesis 3:15 and 1 Peter 1:20. When was salvation planned and promised?
 – Do a word study for *hope* and *redemption*.
 – Read Psalm 130: 3-4 in several translations, then rewrite them in your own words.
 – How do the words in verses 7 and 8 display the psalmist's confident hope in the Lord?
 – Do you have questions about this psalm? Share them with your HM group or a trusted friend.

RESPOND :

. . . .

. . . .

. . . .

. . . .

. . . .

PLAN TIME

THINGS TO DO (3-5 MAX) :

KEY EVENTS TODAY :

MOVE TIME

MORNING WATER ☐

B : _____

L : _____

D : _____

SNACK :

SIMPLE WORKOUT ☐

PART 3, DAY 4: PSALM 8

SOMETIMES I FORGET MY PLACE. I get impatient or even angry with God, forgetting (or at least neglecting to recognize) that He is the sovereign Creator of all things on earth. Do you ever do the same? I think we do this because we forget to praise Him for who He is. Not just for what He has done for us or given to us but simply because He *is* God.

David points out that God's name alone is excellent in all the earth—His name is magnificent, illustrious, and glorious. In Hebrew thought, God's name reveals who He is and the greatness of His character. God's name is better than all other names in all the earth.

We can also begin to understand God's greatness when we realize that He uses the weak things of this earth to display His power and might. When His enemies try to come against Him, the praises from even babes and infants are enough to silence God's foes.

David says that with His fingers—not His arms or His shoulders or His back, but with just His fingers—God created the moon and the stars. David is using figurative language to illustrate the Lord's great strength, creativity, and control over all the universe. From the creation account in Genesis, we know the Lord used less than His fingers. God simply spoke, and His creation came into existence. It was good. It was perfect.

And yet, He is mindful of us. God crowned us with glory and honor because He chose to make us in His image. God made us—who are weaker and lower than the angels, who are prone to disobedient wandering—to have dominion over the works of His hands. God put all things under our feet and gave us authority on earth simply because He wanted to.

This all leads me to further trust God and believe in His love, patience, and kindness towards me. Even though I often forget my place and neglect to revere God for who He is, God is still faithful to me. He doesn't give up on me. He doesn't abandon or neglect. He just keeps on being the good and glorious God that He is.

Lord of all creation, you are worthy of all praise. Please forgive me for forgetting my place and failing to honor and worship you for who you are. Thank you for being patient with me. Loving me and being gentle when I do not deserve it. Thank you for reminding me that I am made in your image and given authority on the earth only because you willed it. I love you. Amen.

—  —

What is man that you are mindful of him, and the son of man that you care for him? (Psalm 8:4)

Hellomornings

God. Plan. Move.

GOD TIME

READ : Psalm 8
WRITE : Psalm 8:4

. . . .

. . . .

. . . .

REFLECT :
- Pray Psalm 8 aloud to your Creator.
- Do a word study for the two different Hebrew words for **Lord** in the first line of verse 1.
- How does the work of God's hand declare His glory?
- What does this psalm reveal about God and about ourselves?
- Do you have questions about this psalm? Share them with your HM group or a trusted friend.

RESPOND :

. . . .

. . . .

. . . .

. . . .

PLAN TIME

THINGS TO DO (3-5 MAX) :

KEY EVENTS TODAY :

MOVE TIME

MORNING WATER ☐

B : _____

L : _____

D : _____

SNACK :

SIMPLE WORKOUT ☐

"LORD, WHO MAY ABIDE IN YOUR TABERNACLE? *Who may dwell in Your holy hill?"* (Psalm 15:1, NKJV) I know I want to. I'm betting you do too; that's why you are taking the time to study God's Word. You know that in order to really know Him, you need to know His thoughts, and His thoughts are written down for us in this great book we call the Bible.

But we want more than to just know Him, don't we? We want to be in His physical presence. We want to see and touch and audibly hear the only One who truly, truly loves us. But is this possible? The list of requirements in order for us to enter His tabernacle and live on His holy hill is long. And I know if I've not met one requirement, then I haven't met any.

Look at the list again. To see God, we must live perfectly—always doing and thinking about what is morally right. We can't gossip, backstab friends, or hold a grudge when they wrong us. We must only despise evil doers (yet simultaneously love them with Christlike love) and must respect those who have a sincere reverence for God. We are to keep our promises, even when we realize doing so will bring ourselves harm. Also, we are not to use our money to take advantage of others or ever take a bribe.

It's a long list, isn't it? And even if we may have been able to meet one or two of the requirements, it doesn't really matter because *"whoever keeps the whole law but fails in one point has become guilty of all of it."* (James 2:10)

So what are we to do? How are we to ascend to the high places and be with God? There is only one thing we can do: place our faith in Jesus Christ, the Son of God. The One who came to earth as a helpless babe, lived a sinless life on our behalf, endured every temptation imaginable, and then gave His life—took our punishment—so that we could experience eternal life in God's presence. But that's not all! He rose from the grave and now sits at the right hand of God, declaring we are His, and our sins are forgiven!

Lord, on my own I am not worthy to abide with you, or dwell on your holy hill. You knew from the beginning that I would not be able to, so you sent your Son to live a blameless life in my place and pay the cost for all my faults and wrongdoings. Your astounding love is worthy of eternal thanksgiving and praise! Amen.

— **KEY VERSE** —

O LORD, who shall sojourn in your tent? Who shall dwell on your holy hill? (Psalm 15:1)

Hellomornings

God. Plan. Move.

GOD TIME

READ : Psalm 15
WRITE : Psalm 15:1

. . . .

. . . .

REFLECT :
- Pray Psalm 15 aloud to your Savior.
- Read Hebrews 2:17-18 and 10:11-23. How do these verses relate to Psalm 15?
- Consider how you have failed to meet the requirements to meet God, yet you are still welcomed into His presence. How can you respond to this mercy and grace?
- What does this psalm reveal about God and about ourselves?
- Do you have questions about this psalm? Share them with your HM group or a trusted friend.

RESPOND :

. . . .

. . . .

. . . .

. . . .

. . . .

PLAN TIME

THINGS TO DO (3-5 MAX) :

KEY EVENTS TODAY :

MOVE TIME

MORNING WATER ☐

B : _____

L : _____

D : _____

SNACK :

SIMPLE WORKOUT ☐

PART 4, DAY 1: PSALM 132

IN MY HOME, I KEEP ONE SEMI-STRICT TRADITION: we do not listen to Christmas carols until *after* Thanksgiving Day. My kids beg for Christmas music all year round, but I stand firm. Part of the reason we love it is it's special! We celebrate Thanksgiving throughout the month of November, focusing on gratitude for the many blessings in our lives, and then the day after (or as soon as it's feasible) we decorate the house for Christmas to a soundtrack of all our favorite holiday songs. The atmosphere in our house and our hearts changes as those familiar tunes fill the air. Memories are stirred and I find myself anticipating the season meant for remembrance of God's sacred gift, when He drew near to us. Music, more than anything else, helps spark a worshipful Christmas spirit.

Psalm 132 belongs to a group of songs with a similar purpose. Traditionally, the Songs of Ascent (Psalm 120 -134) were sung on the upward road to Jerusalem as worshippers made their way to the city for feasts and sacrifices. They may have also been sung by priests as they climbed the steps in the Temple. Even the briefest reading of these fifteen songs reveals a tone of heartfelt worship and a secure hope.

The theme of today's psalm is the covenant the Lord made with David. Imagine the Israelites waiting year after year, sometimes victorious but more often not, desperate for the fulfillment of the Lord's promise for rest and redemption. They recall their hero David, comfortable in his palace, desiring to build a resting place for the Ark. A permanent temple would have solidified the kingdom of Israel, to the people and their neighbors. But the Lord had different ideas. Yes, Jerusalem is His chosen city. Yes, Zion is His resting place. But the kingdom He wanted to establish through David was much bigger than one physical country at one point in history. Through David, He unconditionally promised the Anointed One, who would bring about a new covenant and an eternal kingdom meant for all people.

What a melodious prelude to the incarnation! The Lord of LORDS lowers Himself to the people He created out of dust—people who have broken His heart time and again—and promises to dwell among them, offering community, sustenance, joy, salvation, and glory through the Messiah. Then on a quiet night in a simple town, He becomes a human baby to the poorest of the poor, fulfilling that promise—a son for David's throne, a kingdom eternal.

— **KEY VERSE** —

The Lord swore to David a sure oath from which he will not turn back: One of the sons of your body I will set on your throne. (Psalm 132:11)

GOD TIME

READ : Psalm 132
WRITE : Psalm 132:11

....

....

REFLECT :
- Read the original covenant in 2 Samuel 7. Summarize the promise in your own words.
- Research the places named in Psalm 132:6. How do these images affect the psalm?
- Underline the promises God makes to Zion in verses 13-18.
- What does the Davidic covenant tell us about God's character?
- How is Jesus of Nazareth the fulfillment of the Davidic covenant (see Matthew 21, Luke 1:26-38, and Acts 13:32-39 to get started).

RESPOND :

....

....

....

....

....

PLAN TIME

THINGS TO DO (3-5 MAX) :

KEY EVENTS TODAY :

MOVE TIME

MORNING WATER ☐

B : _____

L : _____

D : _____

SNACK :

SIMPLE WORKOUT ☐

PART 4, DAY 2: PSALM 14

I AM AN AVID FAN OF WHOEVER IT WAS THAT INVENTED THE NIGHTLIGHT. One tiny spot of light in an otherwise dark room and my children feel secure enough to fall asleep. Nothing beats the presence of a parent, but the nightlight helps. Truth be told, I still like to leave a little light on in the kitchen just in case I wake up in the middle of the night. With it, I have a sense of direction. Even from a distance, I can make out the shapes of furniture and walls so I won't (or at least am less likely to) stub sensitive toes.

From the moment Adam and Eve disobeyed the command of the Lord, sin and death darkened the world. It is no stretch of the imagination to picture the fools described in Psalm 14:1-4. We know too well that corrupt politicians, power-hungry corporate leaders, and celebrations of every kind of evil are as prominent today as they have been throughout history.

But there has always been a nightlight; one shining spot of hope providing the security and direction we need to know that the darkness will not overcome. Looking back through Old Testament history, we can see the Lord's plan for redemption unfolding as He builds up the nation of Israel, promising blessings through Abraham, eternal kingship through David, and salvation for the world.

It's not clear exactly when this psalm was written. Some think it was when David was on the run from Saul. This would certainly account for the fools and lawlessness but not necessarily for the hope for salvation from Zion which was under Jebusite control at that time. Others think it may have been inspired by Absalom's rebellion, another dark time in David's life, though now having received the covenant, he has the hope of Zion. Regardless, what is clear is that David understood God's most heartfelt desire to be among His people.

Initially a fortress centrally located in the Promised Land, Zion has come to represent God's Kingdom, established for those who *"...will worship in spirit and in truth..."* (John 4:23). It is the highest point in Jerusalem. It's not in the distance, towering over the land, mysterious and unattainable. It's not the kind of mountain that regular people can only dream of climbing while experts train and plan for perilous expeditions. It's a place God chose to come near, not in power and holy judgement as He had on Mount Sinai, but in humility, grace, and ultimately atonement for our sin.

— KEY VERSE —

Oh, that salvation for Israel would come out of Zion! When the Lord restores the fortunes of His people, let Jacob rejoice, let Israel be glad. (Psalm 14:7)

Hellomornings

God. Plan. Move.

READ : Psalm 14
WRITE : Psalm 14:7

. . . .

. . . .

. . . .

REFLECT :
– What traditional symbols of Christmas point you to spiritual truth?
– Consider what Zion meant to the Jews and what it means to us.
  (https://bible.knowing-jesus.com/topics/Zion,-As-A-Symbol)
– Research the life of David. When might he have written Psalm 14?
– Read Romans 3:9-26. How do these verses apply to Psalm 14?
– Pray for the salvation of the Lord to reach the foolish and corrupt today.

RESPOND :

. . . .

. . . .

. . . .

. . . .

. . . .

PLAN TIME

THINGS TO DO (3-5 MAX) :

KEY EVENTS TODAY :

MOVE TIME

MORNING WATER ☐

B : _____
L : _____
D : _____

SNACK :

SIMPLE WORKOUT ☐

PART 4, DAY 3: PSALM 2

THERE IS A WELL-KNOWN CHRISTMAS CAROL, "Do You Hear What I Hear." My four-year-old doesn't always remember all the words, but she will sing the refrain over and over until I want to cry out, "Yes! I hear what you hear!" Still, I love this song. It's so poetic and has all my favorite Nativity elements—the star, the shepherds, a baby, a prayer for peace...it's almost perfect. But I never could wrap my head around the King. He isn't like the Wise Men (they followed the star) and he most certainly isn't like King Herod. The King in the carol calls for peace and recognizes the child as the One who will bring goodness and light. Herod was more like the earthly kings of Psalm 2, plotting in vain and raging against the Lord's Anointed.

Kingship played a key role in the ancient world. Kings were protectors, statesmen, judges, and often thought to be gods themselves, or at the very least, a high priest. Israel was meant to be a priestly people, set apart and ruled only by the Lord, but they begged for a king so they could be like their Canaanite neighbors. The Lord answered their prayer, first with Saul, who rejected Him, then with David, who loved Him deeply. Under David's reign, the Lord established the Kingdom of Israel and promised an eternal kingdom, ruled by His Anointed One who would be the ultimate High Priest, Judge, Protector, and Supreme King. Psalm 2 almost reads like a retelling of that promise from 2 Samuel 7:14, citing the sonship of the Messiah, the One who would inherit and establish the kingdom of heaven.

Many babies were born in Judea that night, but only Jesus was anointed by the Holy Spirit. We read in Matthew 3:17 when Jesus was baptized, *"...behold, a voice from heaven said, 'This is my beloved Son, with whom I am well pleased,'"* and that the Holy Spirit descended on Jesus like a dove, marking Him as the long-awaited Anointed One spoken of in Psalm 2. John the Baptist said, *"And I have seen and borne witness that this is the Son of God."* (John 1:34).

The earthly kings may plot, but the heir has been anointed, His kingdom established. *"He will bring us goodness and light!"* –Noel Regney

— KEY VERSE —

I will tell of the decree: The Lord said to me, "You are my Son; today I have begotten you." (Psalm 2:7)

Hellomornings

God. Plan. Move.

READ : Psalm 2
WRITE : Psalm 2:7

. . . .

. . . .

. . . .

REFLECT :
- Read 2 Peter 1:17-21. Look up other references to Jesus' anointing (baptism and transfiguration).
- In Acts 4:23-31, Believers pray for boldness. How else can you use Psalm 2 in prayer?
- Research the historical significance of anointing.
- Memorize 1 John 2:20.
- Outline Psalm 2, identifying the Lord's response and command to the kings of the earth.

RESPOND :

. . . .

. . . .

. . . .

. . . .

. . . .

PLAN TIME

THINGS TO DO (3-5 MAX) :

KEY EVENTS TODAY :

MOVE TIME

MORNING WATER ☐

B : _____

L : _____

D : _____

SNACK :

SIMPLE WORKOUT ☐

ON THE FIRST DAY FOLLOWING A THANKSGIVING that we are all home, we haul up way too many boxes of Christmas decorations and make the house over with holiday cheer. The first things we unpack are the Advent wreath and Jesse Tree ornaments. Over the years, I have combined these two traditions into our own unique celebration. Every night, from the start of Advent to Christmas Day, we light the candles and read one of the stories from the Old Testament, specifically those that trace the thread of God's plan to save all of humanity. Then we string a paper ornament representing that story on a garland that wraps around our wreath. On Sundays, we do the same thing, lighting the next candle according to the tradition, until at last the wreath is completely lit. By the time we reach Christmas Eve, we have told the story from creation to the manger many, many times.

It is always so humbling for me to remember that Jesus was God's plan from the beginning. Hebrews 10:1-9 quotes Psalm 40 explaining that the Law, given by Moses, and the sacrificial system practiced by God's people for hundreds of years were only shadows of what was to come in Jesus Christ. *"He does away with the first in order to establish the second."* (Hebrews 10:9)

Peter testified to the crowd in Jerusalem, *"Men of Israel, hear these words: Jesus of Nazareth, a man attested to you by God with mighty works and wonders and signs that God did through him in your midst, as you yourselves know—this Jesus, delivered up according to the **definite plan** and foreknowledge of God, you crucified and killed by the hands of lawless men."* (Acts 2:22-23, emphasis mine).

From the very beginning, God knew we would disobey Him. He orchestrated this great plan, weaving our desperate need for redemption and restoration with His absolute grace throughout history so that when the time came, we could know it was Him all along.

"It takes the whole Bible to tell this Story. And at the center of the Story, there is a baby. Every Story in the Bible whispers his name. He is like the missing piece in a puzzle—the piece that makes the other pieces fit together, and suddenly you can see a beautiful picture." –Sally Lloyd-Jones, *The Jesus Storybook Bible.*

—  KEY VERSE —

Then I said, "Behold, I have come; in the scroll of the book it is written of me." (Psalm 40:7)

Hellomornings

God. Plan. Move.

READ : Psalm 40:1-10
WRITE : Psalm 40:7

. . . .

. . . .

. . . .

REFLECT :

– Write out Deuteronomy 17:18-20. What do these verses have to do with today's passage?
– In verse 2, David speaks of a "pit of destruction" and a "miry bog." What does this imagery call to mind in your own life?
– Consider verse 6. Are there any empty religious practices you need to deal with today?
– Make a list of the wondrous things God has done in your life.
– Summarize God's redemptive plan from creation to the resurrection in your own words.

RESPOND :

. . . .

. . . .

. . . .

. . . .

. . . .

PLAN TIME

THINGS TO DO (3-5 MAX) :

KEY EVENTS TODAY :

MOVE TIME

MORNING WATER ☐

B : _____

L : _____

D : _____

SNACK :

SIMPLE WORKOUT ☐

PART 4, DAY 5: PSALM 40:11-17

"AT THIS FESTIVE SEASON OF THE YEAR, MR SCROOGE, ...many thousands are in want of common necessaries; hundreds of thousands are in want of common comforts, sir." –Charles Dickens, *A Christmas Carol.*

There is nothing like a bright and sparkly holiday celebration to highlight the needs of humanity, whether that is the greater awareness of the poor and hungry or your own grief. Something about seeing another's happiness on full display through holiday cards and perfect social media posts makes your own pain deeper, your discontent heavy. If the first ten verses of Psalm 40 celebrate God becoming a man, the last seven remind me that the story is not over. *"Here is the reflected truth that amid suffering there is joy in God's presence and that amid joy there is continuing human need on earth."* –The *Cambridge Bible Commentary.*

Sin and death were thoroughly defeated by Christ's work on the Cross, but the consequences are still a present reality. As David says, *"For evils have encompassed me beyond number; my iniquities have overtaken me, and I cannot see; they are more than the hairs of my head; my heart fails me."* (v. 12). We are surrounded by broken relationships, prosperity that enslaves, and pain too plentiful to name, never more glaringly obvious than at Christmas.

But the great beauty of the incarnation is that He not only empathizes with our suffering but shares in it completely. Jesus experienced every temptation (Hebrews 4:14-16) and took on the full weight of our sin (2 Corinthians 5:21). If we read verse 13 as His prayer (which we can, as I'll explain in a moment), *"Be pleased, O Lord to deliver me! O Lord, make haste to help me!"* we find it rich with compassion.

Charles Spurgeon described Psalm 40 as *"lifted by the Holy Spirit to the region of prophecy,"* saying, *"David was honored to write concerning far greater than himself."* It's a beautiful mystery that these words, written thousands of years ago, applied to David then, prophesied about Jesus, and are still relevant to today. For just as the Law and the sacrifices of the Old Testament were meant as a shadow to point us to the new covenant, our remembrance of the incarnation serves as a reminder that we are waiting for the time when He comes again. *"So Christ, having been offered once to bear the sins of many, will appear a second time, not to deal with sin but to save those who are eagerly waiting for Him."* (Hebrews 9:28)

— KEY VERSE —

As for me, I am poor and needy, but the Lord takes thought for me. You are my help and my deliverer; do not delay, O my God! (Psalm 40:17)

Hellomornings

God. Plan. Move.

READ : Psalm 40:11-17
WRITE : Psalm 40:17

. . . .

. . . .

. . . .

REFLECT :
- Memorize today's key verse.
- Compare verse 13-17 to Psalm 30. How are they the same? How are they different?
- Are you dealing with any consequences from sin? Ask the Lord for help in bearing them.
- Think about the traditions you celebrate at Christmas. What purpose do they serve?
- Find a way to meet someone's need today. *(http://www.familylife.com/articles/topics/ holidays/featured/christmas/20-ideas-for-serving-others-as-a-family-this-christmas)*

RESPOND :

. . . .

. . . .

. . . .

. . . .

. . . .

PLAN TIME

THINGS TO DO (3-5 MAX) :

KEY EVENTS TODAY :

MOVE TIME

MORNING WATER ☐

B : _____

L : _____

D : _____

SNACK :

SIMPLE WORKOUT ☐

PART 5, DAY 1: PSALM 8

I SCANNED THE FACES FROM MY VIEW FROM THE STAGE. Some wore expressions of joy, others seemed hesitant. Why do some hesitate? In the 20 years I've served as a worship leader, I've considered that same question many times. Worshipping God is our expression of love to Him, an important part of how we interact with Him. Worship reflects our relationship with Him. The hesitation stems from an unclear mindset of how God views His people.

When God created the earth He declared it good. But at the Fall, the seed of sin was sown and sin produces death. We're made in God's image. Sin entered, but it didn't change our image—it changed our position before God (Genesis 6:5-6).

We are revisiting Psalm 8 in this study, this time through the lens of Jesus being the last Adam (1 Corinthians 15:45, 47). From this we can compare the first man, Adam, with Jesus, the Messiah. They are similar in that both represent mankind. Adam, created from the dust of the ground, is made in the image of God; Jesus is the image of the invisible God (Colossians 1:15).

Jesus is the Son of Man, as in son of a human. Why does He have this title? God sent Jesus incarnate to relate to us—as humans. When Jesus came to earth birthed as a baby the same way the rest of us arrive, the event held monumental significance. Not only was He miraculously conceived by the Holy Spirit and born of the virgin Mary, but He arrived to restore His creation as good. Jesus came down from Heaven with a nature both human and divine. Adam, being only human, fell into temptation and disobeyed. Jesus withstood temptation and obeyed the Father, making the way to restore our position before God.

"The healing nature of the cross is not complete without resurrection." –Kenneth Tanner

What makes Jesus the last Adam is not only that He died, but that He rose again. Adam brought death, but Jesus brought life through His resurrection. Spiritually, we have new life in Him now (Romans 6:4). Physically, we are promised the resurrection of the dead in Christ when He returns (1 Thessalonians 4:16). Because of this, we can worship Him, giving Him the honor He's due!

— **KEY VERSE** —

Yet you have made him a little lower than the heavenly beings and crowned him with glory and honor. (Psalm 8:5)

Hellomornings

God. Plan. Move.

READ : Psalm 8
WRITE : Psalm 8:5

....

....

REFLECT :
- Worship God today for restoring your position before Him.
- Make a chart with two columns labeled Adam and Jesus respectively. Refer to the commentary listing the similarities and differences between Adam and Jesus as the last Adam.
- Read the passage again. What does the author begin and end with?
- Look up the cross reference for Psalm 8:2 to find the verse(s) that fulfilled it.
- See John 8:28, 12:32-34, and Matthew 27:50-54. When did the Jews know Jesus is the Messiah?

RESPOND :

....

....

....

....

....

PLAN TIME

THINGS TO DO (3-5 MAX) :

KEY EVENTS TODAY :

MOVE TIME

MORNING WATER ☐

B : _____

L : _____

D : _____

SNACK :

SIMPLE WORKOUT ☐

PART 5, DAY 2: PSALM 32

SLEEPLESS AND STRESSED, I FLIPPED THE COVERS OFF AT 3:00 A.M. and went downstairs to pray. I had worked feverishly for weeks on a project, trying to reach the unrealistic deadline I set for myself. The pace I maintained ravaged sleep and stole family time. The climax transpired in the dark solitude, face-to-face with quiet and no agenda. I wanted to appear like I had it all together when I showed the finished project to people. God showed me the truth: my real problem was pride. I repented, and God forgave me.

Pride is a sin. If this moment had happened in the days before Jesus, according to the Law, sin would be atoned through the shedding of blood—animal sacrifice (Leviticus 1:4). The priest would make sacrifices on my behalf.

The wonderful truth is, I don't have to make an animal sacrifice to receive forgiveness for my sin. I don't have to offer penance to a priest for the remission of sins. I can confess my sins directly to God, and He is faithful and just to forgive my sin and cleanse me from all unrighteousness (1 John 1:9).

Jesus died, becoming the ultimate sacrifice for sins (John 1:29; Hebrews 7:27); animal sacrifice is no longer needed. Remember, He came to earth to restore our position with the Father. Now, because of Jesus, God sees us as righteous!

Psalm 32 was written around the same time as Psalm 51 after David committed adultery with Bathsheba. He *confessed* his sin to God and was forgiven (2 Samuel 12:13). That David, a man after God's heart, started getting glimpses of God's forgiveness that we know of today. *"For you will not delight in sacrifice, or I would give it; you will not be pleased with a burnt offering."* (Psalm 51:16) After that, David gave burnt offerings to God with a heart of worship instead of with a heart fearful of wrong standing (Psalm 51:17,19).

We tend to want to hide our sins—cover them up just like Adam did in the beginning. But Jesus is full of compassion; He forgives. Praise Him for that! In exchange for repentance, God blots out our sins and pours out times of refreshing in His presence.

— KEY VERSE —

I acknowledged my sin to you, and I did not cover my iniquity; I said, "I will confess my transgressions to the LORD," and you forgave the iniquity of my sin. Selah . (Psalm 32:5)

Hellomornings

God. Plan. Move.

GOD TIME

READ : Psalm 32
WRITE : Psalm 32:5

....
....
....

REFLECT :
- Memorize the key verse.
- Does this passage lead you to confess anything in prayer?
- Read today's passage again. Underline any words or phrases that stand out to you.
- David is speaking to man, then God, back to man in today's passage. Observe those changes.
- What other word does the Hebrew use to describe the word blessed in verse 1? (You can find the Interlinear for H835 at *blueletterbible.com*.)

RESPOND :
....
....
....
....
....

PLAN TIME

THINGS TO DO (3-5 MAX) :

KEY EVENTS TODAY :

MOVE TIME

MORNING WATER ☐

B : _____
L : _____
D : _____

SNACK :

SIMPLE WORKOUT ☐

PART 5, DAY 3: PSALM 110

LAST MAY, I BEGAN THE PROCESS OF REDESIGNING MY BLOG. I needed to pick two or three fonts as well as make firm choices on new colors. When I started the redesign journey, I didn't know much about it. As I researched, I put potential color palettes on a list. I consulted Google, talked to other bloggers, asked a friend's opinion, and pinned ideas to a secret board on Pinterest. If you give me 100 choices, I'm lost. Give me three; I can deal with three. Each time I thought I decided on new colors, I checked with my husband. He would share his insights, and I would see them from a new angle and then second-guess myself. My fickleness was ridiculous. It took me weeks before I finally made up my mind.

I'm glad God isn't fickle! Verse four in today's reading tells us the Lord will not change His mind. He is the same yesterday, today, and forever (Hebrews 13:8). God declared that Jesus is a priest forever, appointing Him high priest after the order of Melchizedek.

Why did our Messiah need to be made a priest? Verse one references the enemies of God. When sin entered the world, death entered. Jesus died to break the power of sin and establish the kingdom of God on the earth. The last enemy to be conquered is death (1 Corinthians 15:24-26).

Jesus also holds the offices of King and Judge. In His kingly office, Jesus is now at the right hand of the Father, reigning until the last enemy is overcome (Hebrews 10:12-13). Every principality, power, and rule that opposes Him will be *"made His footstool"* (verse 1); He will conquer them as easily as sliding a footstool under His feet.

"We have seen God incarnate rise up from his three days' sleep to be enthroned as judge of the world. Yet we still await the final fulfillment of Psalms 2, 8, and 110—psalms that both Paul and Hebrews used to express their view of Jesus in the present and their hope for this future coming as judge." –N.T. Wright

I can picture Jesus in such a posture, in His place of authority. Can you? Aren't you glad you serve a God that conquers death? I can't wait until that day!

This Advent, let's praise our constant, faithful, steady, and dependable God.

—  —

The LORD has sworn and will not change his mind, "You are a priest forever after the order of Melchizedek." (Psalm 110:4)

Hellomornings

God. Plan. Move.

READ : Psalm 110
WRITE : Psalm 110:4

. . . .

. . . .

. . . .

REFLECT :
- Write down any questions you have from today's reading. You can answer them later.
- Read Hebrews chapter 7 which expounds on today's reading.
- How does Hebrews 7:26 describe Jesus as high priest?
- Research the difference between an Aaronic priesthood and one after the order of Melchizedek.
- Why did the Father give all judgement to the Son? See John 5:22-23.

RESPOND :

. . . .

. . . .

. . . .

. . . .

. . . .

PLAN TIME

THINGS TO DO (3-5 MAX) :

KEY EVENTS TODAY :

MOVE TIME

MORNING WATER ☐

B : _____

L : _____

D : _____

SNACK :

SIMPLE WORKOUT ☐

PART 5, DAY 4: PSALM 45:1-9

ON MY WEDDING DAY, I planned for my new husband and me to walk through butterflies as our wedding party released them. It was to be the finale on our way to our white chariot—a neighbor's white convertible. Then disappointing news fell the day before our wedding. The lady I asked to be in charge of the butterflies let me know that they had arrived on schedule but weren't emerging. The company where we bought them could do nothing. I didn't want to be pelted with traditional rice; butterflies are softer.

As the minutes decreased to the start hour, problems increased. Finally, one of my dear bridesmaids pulled me aside to let me know that new butterflies had been rush ordered from a different company, and they emerged! The others wanted to surprise me, but she didn't want me to bear the disappointment any longer. Walking through the swirling wonder turned out to be a charming end to our wedding.

Today's reading is a wonderful allegory that represents the Church as the Bride of Christ espoused to our King Jesus. The first half of the psalm is addressed to the groom. The remainder of the psalm is directed to the "bride." We will cover that part in Day 5. Let's look at the "groom" and all He is.

He is handsome (verse 2) because of His purity and love. Although the Bible tells us Jesus was not comely (Isaiah 53:2), His inner beauty shines through His actions. The grace *"poured upon"* his lips is referring to the captivating speech of His Word and promises for us.

"God's beauty is the bouquet of His perfections in His person, unveiled in His purposes, and displayed in His glory." –Steve DeWitt

He is still dressed for battle, ready to subdue His enemies, but He is also wearing fragrant wedding garments (verses 3-5, 8). No more perfect groom exists. He is holy; a lover of righteousness. He is filled with great joy in His duties; we are His joy!(verses 6-7) He is met with His beloved, ready for the imminent nuptials (verse 9).

This royal wedding psalm reminds us how Jesus views His Church—like a groom enraptured with his bride. Oh, how He loves us! One day when He returns, we will unite with Him forever.

— KEY VERSE —

You are the most handsome of the sons of men; grace is poured upon your lips; therefore God has blessed you forever. (Psalm 45:2)

Hellomornings

God. Plan. Move.

READ : Psalm 45:1-9
WRITE : Psalm 45:2

. . . .

. . . .

. . . .

REFLECT :
- How does this mystical marriage redefine your view of Jesus?
- Read the parables that compare the Kingdom of God to marriage: Matthew 22:1-14 and Matthew 25:1-13.
- Who does Hebrews 1:8 reveal Psalm 45:6 is speaking of?
- Make a list of the descriptions of the "groom" in today's reading.
- Read Luke 4:22, a cross reference to the key verse.

RESPOND :

. . . .

. . . .

. . . .

. . . .

. . . .

PLAN TIME

THINGS TO DO (3-5 MAX) :

KEY EVENTS TODAY :

MOVE TIME

MORNING WATER ☐

B : _____

L : _____

D : _____

SNACK :

SIMPLE WORKOUT ☐

AS I BROWSED THROUGH THE MAGAZINE, I didn't realize my habit: assessing the people in the pictures based on their beauty—or lack of it. The Holy Spirit opened my eyes. Had the world's standards so infiltrated my thinking that I stooped to such an appalling practice? With that painful realization, I continued flipping through the magazine. My eyes paused on the next "pretty" woman. *Is she beautiful inside?* Conviction pierced my heart.

I kept flipping, and that's when my eyes saw him—a gruff man with hair much too unkempt for him to be dignified in his crisp suit. Perhaps he turned his lady's head back in the day, but I wanted to look away. *Is he beautiful inside?* I knew God had a lesson for me to learn. I became engrossed in his touching story of a delightful tribute to his uncle. I blinked back the tears with a prayer that God would make my heart as lovely, to see others as He sees us.

The allegory representing the Church as the Bride of Christ espoused to King Jesus continues in today's reading. Notice the directives to the princess in verse ten. She is to hear, consider, incline her ear, and forget her people and father's house. If she is going to marry the king, she is expected to take it seriously. She must worship God alone. He delights in her wholehearted love for Him. She then prepares for the coming ceremony and undergoes a transformation befitting a bride. Once gloriously dressed, she is joyfully escorted to her king.

When I think of a groom, I see a man who is in love with his bride, beaming, excited, and expectant. Jesus is no less; He is already enraptured with His Bride's beauty. In synonymic fashion, references to the bride's beauty represent the holiness of the Church.

"The beauty of holiness, both on the church and on particular believers, is in the sight of Christ of great price and very amiable." –Matthew Henry

Although we can't see inside our hearts, God sees us as beautiful—righteous—because of Christ. As we allow God to renew our spirits daily (2 Corinthians 4:16), He is doing the work to transform us into the holy Bride of Christ to be ready to meet Jesus when He returns (1 Thessalonians 5:23-24).

We need only to love Him with our whole heart—that's true beauty.

—  KEY VERSE —

And the king will desire your beauty. Since he is your lord, bow to him. (Psalm 45:11)

Hellomornings

God. Plan. Move.

READ : Psalm 45:10-17
WRITE : Psalm 45:11

REFLECT :
  – Underline the verbs in Psalm 45:10. Meditate on verse 11.
  – What is God speaking to your heart? Write in your journal how you see Him preparing you to meet Him.
  – Read about the mystery of Christ and the Church in Ephesians 5:25-32.
  – Read Colossians 3:12. Make a list of what we are directed to clothe ourselves with.
  – Tell God you love Him with your whole heart. Praise and thank Him for making you holy.

RESPOND :

PLAN TIME

THINGS TO DO (3-5 MAX) :

KEY EVENTS TODAY :

MOVE TIME

MORNING WATER ☐

B : _____
L : _____
D : _____

SNACK :

SIMPLE WORKOUT ☐

PART 6, DAY 1: PSALM 22:1-18

I REMEMBER STANDING OUTSIDE THAT NIGHT—under the cold, black, star-filled sky. The short walk next door to my parents' house, with a Christmas gift in my hand, should have been totally joyous. But it wasn't. My daughter had been stillborn just a few short weeks prior. There was some Christmas joy in my heart, but it was intertwined with heavy sorrow and grieving. I had gained new understanding of the connection between joy and sadness.

With feet frozen to the barren ground, I prayed for God to show me a mother in the Bible who'd grieved like I did. Immediately, I thought of Mary. The mother of the sweet newborn Babe that grew to offer His life through brutal crucifixion. Knowing Mary must have grieved for her Son gave me the strength to walk across the yard and into the festivities.

In today's psalm, we read King David's words of lament expressing deep trust in God despite rejection. In verses 13 through 18, we read prophetic words about the type of death Jesus endured. This psalm of lament was written about 1,000 years before Christ graced our world, yet foretells in detail a type of death that hadn't yet been invented and would be performed by people who wouldn't even know about this prophecy anyway.

It may seem strange for an Advent study to discuss the crucifixion. The crucifixion is more of a Good Friday message. But what would a celebration of the Light of the World coming to mankind, the great Joy of the World dawning on our hearts be without understanding His purpose in coming? Yes, joy and sadness can be connected.

The beauty of our Babe-in-a-manger's coming is swaddled in the fact that He came for the express purpose of redeeming and ransoming us by offering His life as atonement for our sins. It is by His appearing that we are offered hope, light, and salvation. We rejoice with hearts full of adoration and praise because God looked upon a weary-of-waiting, sin-drenched world and offered us His divine Son to be our ultimate comfort and life-sustaining joy!

So, we read today with the light of understanding only this side of Calvary can give. We read today's psalm with deep gratitude for the immense love our Savior poured out in His death. We read David's words of trust, knowing that God is Holy. As Jesus did throughout His life on earth, we too, can trust God even when birth, life, and death have a strange intertwining.

— KEY VERSE —

But you are holy, O you that inhabits the praises of Israel. (Psalm 22:3)

Hellomornings

God. Plan. Move.

GOD TIME

READ : Psalm 22:1-18
WRITE : Psalm 22:3

. . . .

. . . .

. . . .

REFLECT :
- Read the crucifixion story in John 19 to see how the verses in today's psalm were fulfilled.
- What verses are prophetic in this Messianic psalm?
- Remember, David expresses his feelings in this psalm of lament, yet it is also prophetic. Read commentary on verses 1 and 2.
- Seek out the song "Welcome to our World" by Chris Rice. Worship God through music.
- Is Christmas a painful time for you? Spend time in prayer, thanking God for sending Jesus.

RESPOND :

. . . .

. . . .

. . . .

. . . .

. . . .

PLAN TIME

THINGS TO DO (3-5 MAX) :

KEY EVENTS TODAY :

MOVE TIME

MORNING WATER ☐

B : _____

L : _____

D : _____

SNACK :

SIMPLE WORKOUT ☐

PART 6, DAY 2: PSALM 22:19-26

IN ONE OF MY FAVORITE BOOKS, an utterly evil White Witch claims victory when she slays a mighty lion who gives his life to save a sordid, sulky boy. After the deed was done, the Witch's vile minions shouted in hate-filled triumph and raised their fists to the sky while she haughtily gazed over the scene. They thought they'd conquered their enemy. What they didn't realize was that the life-sacrificing, love-giving lion had the power to conquer death itself. In a powerful shift and surprise, he rose again!

Today's passage contains a surprising shift. Like the story of the lion and witch, yesterday's sorrowful passage points to a sacrificial death. And if we weren't living on this side of the resurrection, we might think we'd been defeated. But as we read today's passage, our hearts do an about-face from lamenting (albeit, with gratitude) toward *praise* for the Lord's victorious triumph!

In verses nineteen through twenty-one, David expresses the desire for salvation from the enemy. (Though David penned this *Psalm of the Cross,* the words are considered by Biblical scholars to directly reflect Christ upon the cross.) And we know Christ was triumphant over the enemy! It was through His obedient death and powerful resurrection that He proved Himself victorious.

And in that knowledge, we praise. Like in verses 22 through 26, our hearts can't help but praise Him for all He's done for us. Through His affliction, He washed away the sin that afflicts *us*. And He hasn't hidden from us, but has heard us when we cry out to Him (verse 24). He came to love and save. Reasons for praise abound!

Christmas is a celebration. Our gratitude for all He's done is coupled with *great joy*. So, we publically display love returned to God for His greatly loving us! Our praise is poured out as a sacrifice as we celebrate His triumph. And rightly so; He wants us to share His message and His name with the world (see verse 22 and His post resurrection words, *"go tell my brothers"* in Matthew 28:10).

Today's passage shows gratitude expressed by both a sacrifice and a feast. So, as we celebrate Christmas, let's keep our eyes planted firmly on Jesus—our ultimate sacrifice. His death and resurrection prove He is King forever! (verse 28) And just as we need food, we need Him. He is our feast—body and blood, true manna and wine (see verse 26.) Our Savior was born to rise again. Death is conquered and His work is complete!

— KEY VERSE —

I will tell of your name to my brothers; in the midst of the congregation I will praise you. (Psalm 22:22)

Hellomornings

God. Plan. Move.

GOD TIME

READ : Psalm 22:19-26
WRITE : Psalm 22:22

. . . .

. . . .

. . . .

REFLECT :

– Read the remainder of this psalm which describes millennial blessings.
– Read Hebrews 2:12. What is the connection between that passage and today's key verse?
– What insight does John 6:53-58 give us to Psalm 22:26?
– Research the first and last words of Christ on the cross. Find them in this psalm.
– Consider gathering friends or family to watch the allegorical movie *The Chronicles of Narnia: The Lion, the Witch, and the Wardrobe*. Pray and praise God for His gift of Jesus!

RESPOND :

. . . .

. . . .

. . . .

. . . .

. . . .

PLAN TIME

THINGS TO DO (3-5 MAX) :

KEY EVENTS TODAY :

MOVE TIME

MORNING WATER ☐

B : _____

L : _____

D : _____

SNACK :

SIMPLE WORKOUT ☐

PART 6, DAY 3: PSALM 16

WHEN MY GRANDPARENTS PASSED AWAY, their belongings were sorted through. I remembered their beautiful glass salt and pepper shakers shaped like corn cobs that hung from a bright silver stand. I had fond memories of breakfast at my grandparents', so I asked for them. But when my little "inheritance" came, I was surprised. The glass and silver were actually faded plastic and the lids didn't screw on correctly. I still cherished them for the years they lasted, but I knew their quality affected their longevity.

In today's psalm of trust, written by David, we read about a superior inherited gift—one that won't disappoint! Because God had empowered David to slay a giant, preserved his life from enemies, given him the kingship over Israel, and faithfully shepherded him throughout his life, David knew God's character was completely trustworthy. God was David's all in all.

And not only did David trust God to be his life's portion, but he also trusted God to preserve him in death! Verses 9 through 11 expound on this. Look carefully at verse 10. Though David penned these words of trust in God's granting eternal life to mankind, the words aren't just about us; they are prophetic of Christ! (See Acts 13:35.) Christ would not see corruption, but instead was resurrected from the dead, just like we talked about yesterday.

Yes, it's because of Jesus and the sweet Christmas story we are guaranteed an inheritance. Not one that doesn't last (like my salt and pepper shakers), but an incorruptible, spiritual one where we will be reunited with the One who died for us. Our beautiful inheritance is the solid hope of eternity with Jesus. And that changes the way we look at life each day.

And our hope never disappoints us! The proof is in the Holy Spirit. See, when my Christian grandparents passed away it meant *earthly* separation from their children and grandchildren. But Christ's death is different; it does not mean any separation from His children. Instead, God comes in the form of the Holy Spirit to dwell in all Believers. This is a down payment on our eternity (Ephesians 1:14) and is the absolute proof of the truth of the "beautiful inheritance" we read about in this psalm.

By belief in the joyfully adored baby King Jesus as our Lord, (Romans 10:9) we are promised eternal life with Him and an eternal weight of glory beyond all comparison. This Christmas, let's aim to be like David and "set the Lord always before me." (Psalm 16:8)

—  KEY VERSE —

LORD, You are my portion and my cup of blessing; You hold my future. (Psalm 16:5 HCSB)

Hellomornings

God. Plan. Move.

GOD TIME

READ : Psalm 16
WRITE : Psalm 16:5

. . . .

. . . .

. . . .

REFLECT :
- Choose a verse from today's passage to meditate on.
- Read through this psalm again. Underline anything that stands out to you.
- Read 2 Corinthians 4:16–5:5. What does this passage teach us about our eternity?
- Make a list of attributes of God that give you a reason to place your hope in Him.
- Pray that God would show you people that need to be reminded (or taught) of His goodness this Christmas. Pray for opportunities to reach the unsaved.

RESPOND :

. . . .

. . . .

. . . .

. . . .

PLAN TIME

THINGS TO DO (3-5 MAX) :

KEY EVENTS TODAY :

MOVE TIME

MORNING WATER ☐

B : _____

L : _____

D : _____

SNACK :

SIMPLE WORKOUT ☐

PART 6, DAY 4: PSALM 118:1-13

MY TEENAGE DAUGHTER OFTEN TEACHES ME how to do things on the newer social media apps. She sent me a video recently with a really cool effect. Words were "pasted" over her mouth and moved when she moved! I had no idea that could be done. It made me think of how sometimes with God we limit Him to what we think is possible.

Psalm 118 is a Messianic Psalm that points to Christ as the cornerstone of our faith. Though we aren't sure who wrote this beautiful song of thanksgiving and trust, some scholars suggest that it was David or perhaps another high official set in place by the Lord. Either way, what we do know is that this psalm has both prophetic content and encouragement for us today.

Over and again in this song sung by worshippers heading to the Temple, the psalmist shows us the strength of his faith. Though surrounded by his enemies, he trusts that God will deliver him. (Psalm 118:6) He doesn't foolishly place his trust in chariots and princes.

Though I'll never be sure if this psalm was written by David, I can't help but think of faith like David's when he went up against Goliath. David put no limits on God's power. Though small, unarmed, and not trained for war, He knew God was *abundantly* able to save him from the mighty giant and to save Israel from the Philistines. (See 1 Sam 17.)

Like David and this unnamed psalmist, we shouldn't put limits on God either. After all, look at God's complex but simple plan of redemption. The miraculous birth of His Son to a sweet, young virgin proves that His abilities are limitless!

Though we may not have any physical enemies like the leaders of Israel did, we certainly have our struggles. We must remember that our powerful Lord, in His enduring love and mercy, can conquer our "enemies" too. Christ came to set us free. *Our God is greater* than our worries, pain, and temptations. Yes, we may struggle, but He spiritually delivers.

That was the point of why God sent a precious baby, laid in a manger—to offer us the spiritual victory of eternal salvation. Though the Lord may or may not chose to deliver us physically in this life, we are always delivered spiritually. Like David, we must place our complete faith and trust in Him. We can take heart that He has proven Himself worthy of our doing just that!

—  —

It is better to trust in the Lord than to put confidence in man. (Psalm 118:8)

Hellomornings

God. Plan. Move.

READ : Psalm 118:1-13
WRITE : Psalm 118:8

. . . .

. . . .

. . . .

REFLECT :
– What does this passage tell us about God?
– What insight does this passage give about mankind?
– Look up the Hebrew word for *mercy* used in this psalm. What did you discover?
– What enemies, foes, or struggles do you have? Make a list and pray through them.
– Thank the Lord today that He is worthy of our praise and trust!

RESPOND :

. . . .

. . . .

. . . .

. . . .

. . . .

PLAN TIME

THINGS TO DO (3-5 MAX) :

MOVE TIME

MORNING WATER ☐

B : _____

L : _____

D : _____

KEY EVENTS TODAY :

SNACK :

SIMPLE WORKOUT ☐

ON LONG WINTER NIGHTS GROWING UP, my brother and I would often amuse ourselves by playing dominoes. Sometimes afterwards, we'd start building things. Later, we'd slowly pull pieces out of our designs, anxiously waiting to see when it would all fall apart. It only took a few pulls to see which piece was the "cornerstone," without which the whole thing would collapse.

In today's reading, we again read prophetic words about Jesus. Interestingly, Jesus Himself most likely sang these very psalm lyrics during the Passover meal that He celebrated with His disciples the night before His death. (See Matthew 26:30.) Psalms 113 through 118 are all part of what is called the Passover Hallel and it was Jewish custom to read or sing these psalms as part of the Passover celebration. Imagining God in human flesh singing the beautiful, sad words of this psalm about Himself is precious and bittersweet to me.

The first verse in today's passage mentions that the Lord has become the psalmist's salvation. The word used here is a form of the word *yeshuah*. Jesus' very own name, Yeshua in Hebrew, comes from this verb meaning to *save, deliver*. Essentially, this passage points to Yeshua, Jesus, our great Savior and Deliverer who came without grandeur or laud. Likewise the same word, *yeshuah*, is used in Isaiah 12:3 which tells of drawing water from the "wells of salvation." There is no other way to access salvation than through Christ, who *is* our salvation!

The focus of verses 22 and 23 is the day when the cornerstone would be established. Yes, Christ, the well of our salvation, is our mighty cornerstone—our Rock! Since it's crucial to the integrity of the building, much depends on this stone being strong. Christ applied this exact passage to Himself in Matthew 21:42-44. He claims that *He* is our foundation. If we were to foolishly pull Christ from His rightful position in our hearts, all would come crashing down.

Though we were once held captive to sin, Christ has redeemed and delivered us, and reconciled us to God. Our *salvation,* our *cornerstone,* our Emmanuel has come! Indeed, we can give thanks to the Lord at Christmastime and always because His mercy endures forever! *Thank you, Jesus!*

"The Spirit of the Lord is upon me, because he has anointed me to proclaim good news to the poor. He has sent me to proclaim liberty to the captives and recovering of sight to the blind, to set at liberty those who are oppressed." (Luke 4:18)

— **KEY VERSE** —

The stone which the builders rejected has become the cornerstone. (Psalm 118:22)

Hellomornings

God. Plan. Move.

READ : Psalm 118:14-29
WRITE : Psalm 118:22

. . . .

. . . .

REFLECT :
– What does this passage specifically prophesy about Jesus?
– Read about Christ's offer of living water: *www.donotdepart.com/jesus-offers-us-living-water*.
– Do you know what a cornerstone is? Look up the definition. How is Christ a cornerstone?
– How does this passage prepare your heart for celebrating Christmas?
– As you give and open gifts soon, thank God for the gift He has given us—the gift of His Son, Jesus. Thank Him for being the cornerstone, the deliverer, and a well of salvation.

RESPOND :

. . . .

. . . .

. . . .

. . . .

. . . .

PLAN TIME

THINGS TO DO (3-5 MAX) :

KEY EVENTS TODAY :

MOVE TIME

MORNING WATER ☐

B : _____
L : _____
D : _____

SNACK :

SIMPLE WORKOUT ☐

CONCLUSION

SO MUCH CAN HAPPEN SO QUICKLY! Does it seem like a long time ago that we started this journey together? We've trekked from heartfelt gratitude to celebrating Jesus and perhaps understanding a little more about His life and the purpose of His coming. As we discussed in the Introduction to this study, whether we feel we have a little or a lot, we have much to be thankful for. With Him we have everything — He is our all in all!

I hope you've enjoyed studying these beautiful poems together and worshipping, praying, learning from, and rejoicing right along with the original writers of these ancient hymns. I am thankful that God chose to author Scripture through the pens of these various writers who loved and cherished God so greatly.

I pray that when you close the pages of this book and go off to join your family in celebrating Christmas, your heart will be overflowing with fresh adoration and renewed appreciation for our God and His Son, Jesus. I pray that you'll be praising His name greatly, for He is Greatly to Be Praised!

May our Lord ever be magnified in our hearts and lives!

In Him,

Ali

ALI SHAW can't believe how blessed life is! As a Central Texas wife, momma, and new grandma, Ali leads a full, grace-filled life. She serves as the HelloMornings Bible Study Director and owns and writes for *DoNotDepart.com* and is generally in awe that God will use a regular girl like her! Woven with practical insight, her writing encourages women to seek God daily through the reading and study of His Word. Most of her writing can be found through HelloMornings or DoNotDepart, but she blogs occasionally at her personal blog, *HeartfeltReflections.wordpress.com* where she's written an online Bible study, Learning from Job. She has also authored an in depth Bible study of Abigail. For information or encouragement, you can connect with her on Facebook at *facebook.com/heartfeltreflectionsblog*.

For **COURTNEY COHEN,** everything comes down to two questions: *Who is God?* and, *Who has He designed us to be?* Whether she's writing, speaking, or homeschooling her children, these questions propel her forward. Author of multiple books including *The Sacred Shadow* and *Refining Identity*, Courtney passionately helps people encounter the reality and nearness of God in everyday life. Courtney is married to Steve, her most radical supporter, who also keeps her real. Together, they co-founded and serve at Now Found Ministries. Living in Texas, Courtney and Steve have three children who, simultaneously, bless her socks off and keep her on her toes. Stay in touch with Courtney at *NowFound.org*.

JAIME HILTON is 1/6 of the Hilton Family in Lancaster, Pennsylvania. She is the household manager and wife to Ray, the actor. Together they are in the trenches of parenting four children, ages 2-14. Thanks to homeschooling and her voracious reading habits, she has her library card number memorized. In her (rare!) spare time she likes to write and work with local theater companies, directing and encouraging fellow artists to glorify God in every aspect of their work. Her favorite mornings start with a quiet cup of coffee and an inspiring book or blog. Her most passionate pursuit is studying the Word and discovering the stories within The Story. She blogs from time to time about life, homeschool, and theater at *allthewordlastage.org* and is active on Facebook @jaime.hilton.

KELLI LAFRAM is actually Kelli LaFramboise, but no one can pronounce that, so with the permission of her husband and four kids she writes under the shorter pen name. Her neighbors have started referring to her bunch as the LaFram Fam. In addition to writing for Hello Mornings, Kelli has also led bible studies in her home and served in the children's ministry at her local church. Kelli is an elementary school teacher and her hobbies include blogging about God's word, listening to audiobooks with her children, drinking good coffee, hand painting faith-based signs (but not after too much coffee), and helping her carpenter husband build furniture. You can find her at *quietlyreminded.com*, *facebook.com/KelliLaFram/*, and *instagram.com/kellilafram/*.

KELLY R. BAKER is passionate about helping you seek God daily and thrive. She has created several resources on her website to inspire you to keep moving forward in spiritual growth such as the *Daily Time with God Challenge* and *40 Days of Daily Bread: Devotionals for Breakthrough*. In addition to being a writer, she serves with her husband in leading the worship ministry at their church in northern Virginia. When not keeping her four kids on the homeschool and household routine, you will probably find her sneaking a bite (or two) of organic dark chocolate. She would rather

be writing or watching chick flicks than shopping any day. Connect with her on Facebook @kellyrbakerdotcom and Twitter @liveyielded. Find her at *kellyrbaker.com*.

PATTI BROWN lives with her husband and three kids in rural Texas, where they make lots of messes while they sing, write, act, knit, and invent new recipes. When she is not homeschooling or cleaning up those messes, she is a local women's ministry leader and a writer. Meeting Jesus in His Word, and trying to walk in obedience to it, has transformed her life, and made her passionate about encouraging women to study the Bible. You can find Patti writing regularly with a team of authors at *donotdepart.com*, and occasionally on her blog at *joyfulmama.com*. She joined her first HelloMornings challenge in November of 2010 and was blessed to work in leadership with HelloMornings for three years. Greatly to Be Praised is the sixth HelloMornings Bible study to which Patti has contributed.